Renaissance Profiles

Renaissance Profiles

GARRETT MATTINGLY   MORRIS BISHOP

RALPH ROEDER   KENNETH CLARK

IRIS ORIGO   J. BRONOWSKI

DENIS MACK SMITH   H. R. TREVOR-ROPER

MARIA BELLONCI

EDITED BY
J. H. PLUMB

HARPER TORCHBOOKS
Harper & Row, Publishers
New York, Hagerstown, San Francisco, London

RENAISSANCE PROFILES

Copyright © 1961 by American Heritage Publishing Co. Inc.

This book was first published in *The Horizon Book of the Renaissance* in 1961 by American Heritage Publishing Company, and is here reprinted by arrangement

First HARPER TORCHBOOK edition published 1965 by
Harper & Row Publishers, Incorporated
10 East 53rd Street
New York, N.Y., 10022

Library of Congress catalog card number: 61-11489

ISBN: 0-06-131162-6

83 84   20

Contents

I.

Petrarch

by MORRIS BISHOP

"I was born to this world," says Petrarch, "in the Via dell' Orto of the City or Arezzo, just at dawn on Monday, July 20, in the thirteen hundred and fourth year of this latest age which takes its name from Jesus Christ, fountain and author of all my hope." The house of his birth still stands at the town's top, across from the cathedral. Houses occupied by great ghosts live long.

He was christened Francesco Petracco, a slightly inelegant name which he Latinized to Petrarca, which we have Anglicized to Petrarch.

He was an Aretine only by circumstance. His father, Ser Petracco, was an office-holding notary, or attorney, in Florence, living on the edge of poverty. He belonged to the bourgeois party of the Whites; and in the revolution of 1302 he was banished, together with Dante and many others, and took refuge in Arezzo, some sixty miles away. But as Arezzo gave a chill welcome to plotting Florentine exiles, Ser Petracco had soon to seek his fortune afar. His wife, Eletta, and baby were permitted to return to the family house in Incisa, on Florentine territory.

According to a dear family story, Francesco, seven months old, was transported to Incisa in a sort of sling depending from a stout

1

stick borne over a mounted servant's shoulder. In fording the flooded Arno, the horse slipped and fell; the servant nearly lost his life in saving that of the child. This is the kind of incident that has made Fortune a deity.

In Incisa was born, in 1307, Francesco's brother Gherardo, the product of a furtive visit of Ser Petracco. In 1310 or 1311 the family was reunited for a year in Pisa, and there, or possibly in Genoa, Ser Petracco was visited by his old friend and fellow exile Dante. By this time Ser Petracco found a post in the papal court, which had removed from Rome to Avignon. There, in 1312, his wife and sons joined the exile.

Avignon was a town of some five thousand inhabitants. The arrival of the papal court affected it as would the establishment of the United Nations in a rural American county seat. Cardinals' trains were billeted in citizens' homes, petitioners and office seekers camped in the streets, on the walls, in cemeteries. Signora Petracco and the boys found lodgings in the town of Carpentras, fifteen miles away, and there they spent four happy years. Writing, years later, to Guido Sette, a schoolmate and a lifelong friend, Petrarch remembered in Carpentras only joy, security, peace at home, liberty in public, and country silence round about. He recalled tenderly how the boys watched out the night in talk on the eternal subjects. He remembered also that while his companions were studying their Latin for grammatical and rhetorical lessons, "I was noting down the substance of thought—the pettiness of this life, its brevity, haste, tumbling course, its hidden cheats, time's irrecoverability, the flower of life soon wasted, the fugitive beauty of a blooming face, the flight of youth, the trickeries of age, the wrinkles, illnesses, sadness, and pain, and the implacable cruelty of indomitable death." Already he was oppressed by the sense of time and its hurry toward the end.

One day his father came to Carpentras with Guido Sette's uncle. Despite Signora Petracco's fears, they visited the famous Fontaine de Vaucluse, fourteen miles away. Francesco was enchanted with the lovely rocky gorge and with the fountain itself, a mysterious swirling pool, where long-hidden underground waters furiously emerge under limestone cliffs. This, he said, was the place he would most wish to live, rather than in any great city.

Francesco, Gherardo, and Guido Sette were sent to the University of Montpellier and then to Bologna, to study law. Seven wasted years, Francesco called them, but although he detested the law—the art of selling justice—he had time to read widely in the classics, to perfect his Latin style, and to correct his Italian not far from the Tuscan fount. He loved fat Bologna, *pinguis Bononia,* its songs and its dances; he loved also to escape on feast days for long country walks, returning after dark to climb the crumbling walls.

The parents died, and Francesco and Gherardo returned, in 1326, to Avignon. Francesco always maintained that his guardians robbed him of his small property, an act which reinforced his dislike of the law. He refused to practice—"I couldn't face making a merchandise of my mind," he said—but he must have had some employment at the papal court, for he and his brother led the life of elegant young men about town.

Francesco was tall and active, with a clear complexion, between light and dark, keen, lively eyes, and reddish-brown hair, which turned prematurely gray, to his great grief. He was vain of his good looks. He later recalled to Gherardo how the pair of them would work all night on their coiffures, sometimes burning their brows with curling irons, how they would dispose every fold of their gowns, terrified lest wind should discompose them and horses splash them with mud; and he recalled his very long, very tight boots, which would have crippled him if he had not revolted in time. He remembered their stylish talk, with dislocated words and dropped syllables, and their popularity, their swarms of visitors, and the vain, lewd songs they sang. He wrote poetry in the current mode, which he was later careful to destroy, and he had more than his share of amorous success with the light women who followed the papal court.

On April 6, 1327, when he was not yet twenty-three, he attended the early morning office at the church of St. Clare. There and then for the first time he saw Laura, and there and then the god Amor's arrow pierced his heart and made a wound never to be staunched.

To rid himself of Laura's obsessing image, he says, he traveled far. But again he says that the real reason was a great inclination and longing to see new sights. He got as far as Paris, Flanders, Germany, Rome; he would have liked to push on to the farthest Indies, to Tarprobane. Even in old age he loved to travel on a map, with the aid of books and imagination. He has been called the first tourist, journeying for pleasure alone; and indeed it is hard to thing of a predecessor, for even Herodotus wandered with a book in view.

For pleasure alone he climbed Mont Ventoux, which rises to more than six thousand feet, beyond Vaucluse. It was no great feat, of course; but he was the first recorded Alpinist of modern times, the first to climb a mountain merely for the delight of looking from its top. (Or almost the first; for in a high pasture he met an old shepherd, who said that fifty years before he had attained the summit, and had got nothing from it save toil and repentance and torn clothing.) Petrarch was dazed and stirred by the view of the Alps, the mountains around Lyons, the Rhone, the Bay of Marseilles. He took Augustine's *Confessions* from his pocket and reflected that his climb was merely an allegory of aspiration toward a better life.

To qualify for the right to receive income from church benefices he took the tonsure, which commited him to nothing much (though ruining his stylish coiffure). Aided, no doubt, by wealthy patrons, he bought a small house in the picturesque gorge of Vaucluse, thus linking forever the names of Petrarch, Laura, and Vaucluse. His retreat was only twenty miles from the hateful city of Avignon, the Western Babylon, with its traffic noise, its scavenging pigs and dogs, and its filthy dust blown by the mistral. When he went to town he tried to make himself insensible, but he had much business in Avignon, for he was already well known as a poet and scholar, and of course Laura was there.

If he did not exactly discover the love of wild nature, he established it as a literary convention for all later times. His beautiful descriptions of country sights and sounds, of the little Sorgue, with its crystal waters and the emerald luster of its bed, moved and still move the poetic imagination of the Western world. But his solitude was laborious. "I rise at midnight, leave the house at dawn; and in the fields I study, think, write, and read. I fight off sleep as long as I can, and keep dainties from the body, pleasures from the soul, sloth from my behavior. All day I wander on bare mountains, dewy valleys, and in mossy caves, alone with my thoughts." He lived simply. A servant once asked him, "What do you eat?" "Polenta, toasted turnips, greens, vegetables, sometimes delicious cows' milk." "No meat?" "I'm not a wolf that feeds on flesh."

He worked fruitfully, producing, in Italian, poems of love's longing and despair, which were passed from literary hand to hand, with copies taken on the way. They were diffused throughout Italy, sung to the lute in such gatherings of gentlefolk as Boccaccio describes. In Latin he wrote giant compendiums of ancient learning, an epic poem which was to rival Virgil's, and endless enchanting letters. His retreat was not a rejection of the world; it was a roundabout means of attaining worldly fame.

This he gained. For him Rome revived its ancient custom of crowning a poet with symbolic laurel. On April 8, 1341, on the holy ground of Rome's Capitol, he became the first laureate of modern times. His celebrity spread far: an old blind poet from near Genoa had himself led, and often carried, by his son to Naples, in order to hear and feel the presence of his idol. Missing Petrarch there, the pilgrims pursued him to Parma, and for three days blessed God for their companionship with poetic divinity.

The attainment of one's ambition is always disillusioning, or so we are told. Petrarch's sense of human vanity and void increased; he went through a period of crisis. His dear brother Gherardo, shocked by the death of the woman he loved, entered a Carthusian monastery, to spend a six-year novitiate in virtual silence. Was not this, indeed, the better way? In his self-questioning mood Petrarch wrote a beautiful series of penitential psalms, and also his extraordinary *Secretum*. This, his secret book, never revealed during his life, is a dialogue with Saint Augustine. The saint, with robust assurance, explores Petrarch's character and faults and brings to light his subconscious motives. He berates Petrarch for his sensuality, his overweening love of fame, his really ridiculous sighing for unattainable Laura, and his *accidia,* or fits of un-reasoning gloom. "Give yourself back to yourself!" says the saint. The little book, stemming from Augustine's own *Confessions,* is the first example of introspective self-analysis of modern times.

His sensuality bore its fruit. He had a son, Giovanni, born in 1337, and a daughter, Francesca, born in 1343. Whether there was one mother or two we do not know. Petrarch did his best for his children. He had them legitimized, gave the son the best education obtainable, and procured for him an ecclesiastical living; but the boy was a sad scapegrace, at least in the father's eyes. He died at the age of twenty-four, in the Plague of 1361. The girl, on the other hand, was the consolation of Petrarch's later years.

From 1343 onward Petrarch spent more and more of his time in Italy, partly because he obtained comfortable canonicates there, partly because Vaucluse had nearly served its purpose, and partly because he enjoyed implication in great affairs. In Parma, during the Great Plague of 1348, he learned that his Laura had died on the sixth of April, twenty-one years to the hour from the moment he had first seen her in the church of St. Clare. (The coinci-dence is astounding; whether too astounding for belief depends on one's capacity for belief.) He lived for a time in Padua; he visited Florence and was triumphally received. The city restored his family property to him; but as he did not immediately make his residence there, it took the property back again. He returned for two years to Vaucluse. After his departure, his house was robbed of everything except his books; he never saw it again. He settled in Milan, city of the Visconti tyrants, hateful to all Florentines. For this he was much blamed even by his best friends; and indeed it does seem a surrender to an ambition he affected to despise. He served the Visconti as envoy to Venice and to the Emperor Charles IV, and he made an official trip to Paris to felicitate the blood-thirsty King John the Good of France on his release from an English prison.

In Milan, in 1359, he received a visit from Boccaccio, nine years his junior. The two became fast friends; their precious correspondence is a literary treasure. (Petrarch left Boccaccio, in his will, money to buy a warm dressing gown for "winter study and lucubrations by night.")

Restless, he left Milan in 1361 for varying stays in Pavia, Padua, and Venice. The city of Venice gave him a palazzo on the Riva degli Schiavoni, whence he could watch the ships setting forth for the Black Sea and Egypt and the Holy Land. In return, he offered his books to the city, expecting them to be the nucleus of the first public library since ancient times. (But after his death they were not delivered; at least twenty-six of them arrived, after centuries of adventure, in Paris.)

Venice did not satisfy him; nothing satisfied him. Four young Aristotelians visited him, and made clear that they thought him an old fogey. He was shocked by a cleric à la mode, who praised only Averroes, and called Paul and Augustine and the rest a lot of gabblers. He was inspired to write the treatise *On His Own Ignorance and That of Many Others.*

He was old and tired and conscious of being out of date. He removed to Padua and bought a country house at Arquà in the hills to the southward. It still stands, in its olive groves and vineyards, flower-framed, bird-beloved, as in his day. His daughter Francesca joined him. She had married well; her son Francesco was the image of his grandfather. The child's death at the age of two nearly broke the old man's heart. "I never loved anything on earth as I loved him," he grieved, but he came to love no less his winsome granddaughter Eletta, named for his mother.

Illness gathered: fevers, fainting spells, foot trouble, and the itch. He was so thin that he was afraid of vanishing. Boccaccio urged him to take things easy, to stop writing. "No," he said; "nothing weighs less than a pen, and nothing gives more pleasure; it is useful not only to the writer but to others far away, perhaps even to those who will be born a thousand years from now."

In the morning of July 19, 1374, he was found dead at his writing desk, the pen dropped from his hand on his *Life of Julius Caesar.* (But some distrust this story, too exquisitely apt.) He lacked a day of reaching seventy years, the Psalmist's span.

"What am I?" he had asked himself, a few years before. "A scholar? No, hardly that; a lover of woodlands, a solitary, in the habit of uttering disjointed words in the shadow of beech trees, and used to scribbling presumptuously under an immature laurel tree; fervent in toil, but not happy with the results; a lover of letters, but not fully versed in them; an adherent of no sect, but very eager for truth; and because I am a clumsy searcher, often, out of self-distrust, I flee error and fall into doubt, which I hold in lieu of truth. Thus I have finally joined that humble band that knows nothing, holds nothing as certain, doubts everything—outside of the things that it is sacrilege to doubt."

Petrarch is important to us in three ways—as a poet, as a humanist scholar, and as a living human being.

The irruption of Laura—or love's reality—into Petrarch's life turned him from a rhymester in the prevailing mode into a great poet.

Who was Laura, his muse? Some have doubted if she ever existed. They point to the Provençal convention that a poet must sigh forever for an unattainable lady, to Petrarch's presumed desire to outdo Dante's mystical love for Beatrice in his *Viva Nuova,* to the discord between Petrarch's proclaimed devotion for Laura and his simultaneous gross amours, and to the convenient triple meanings of the word *Laura: il lauro,* or the poetic laurel; *l'aura,* the zephyr; *l'auro,* gold. Laura, they say, is merely an allegory, a useful fiction.

No, Laura was a real woman. Many efforts have been made to track her down. The identification with Laure de Sade, née Laure de Noves, is very old, and while it presents difficulties, it is not at all unlikely. An identification is not, perhaps, very important, but readers always want to know how much is true in any fiction, as writers are usually reluctant to tell.

His *Rime in Vita e Morte di Madonna Laura,* 366 poems (the

leap-year number), give us plenty of specific facts. Laura was young, golden-haired, noble, rich; she came from the hill country near Vaucluse, and she was married and settled in Avignon. She was one of a group of young matrons who went bathing and boating together. Many of the poems take their rise from an incident—the poet's attempt to purloin a glove; an eye affliction of Laura's; a new dress, purple with pink spots, blue-bordered, reminding the poet of phoenix feathers.

We have other evidence of her reality. In Petrarch's *Secretum,* his private, undivulged self-examination Saint Augustine sneers that Laura's body, worn out by illness and frequent childbirths, has lost its old beauty. Petrarch admits the fact, but protests that she cleansed his youthful soul of all filth and taught him to look upwards. "Nonsense!" says Augustine, a hardheaded confessor. "She has ruined your life! She turned you from the love of the Creator to the love of the creature!" Augustine makes his charge admit that Laura's youthful beauty, and her significant name, allured the poet, and that he had besieged her with his sensual desires. "But she never yielded!" protests Petrarch. "I could never love anything else! My soul is so used to adoring her, my eyes so used to gazing on her, that all is not she looks dark and ugly!"

What exactly did he want? He is always pleading in his poems for "pity," for "yielding," for the gift of mercy forever sought by the Provençal poets. One may amuse oneself by imagining that one day she might have decided to "yield." How he would have fled! She would have ruined his whole book.

Long, hopeless fidelity is the poet's best theme. But it has to be sincere, it has to be true. Then it has to be converted into beautiful poetic form. Every reader of Petrarch's poems must feel their truth and must recognize their beauty.

His commonest device was to take an incident of the endless courtship and develop it in sonnet form into a "conceit," or a fancy, or a coherent rounded thought. Some of the conceits are very thin-spun, elaborate, on the edge of absurdity. The form was enthusiastically adopted by the poets of Italy, France, and England, and the Petrarchan sonnet gained a universal vogue which eventually brought upon it nearly universal scorn. (But the "conceit" has returned to poetry today.) The fading of the Petrarchan tradition has left in many minds an aversion from Petrarch, wholly undeserved, for much of his poetry is simple, straightforward, expressing a deep emotion in everyday words which magically turn to lovely harmonies.

Instead of describing unknown, unread poems, let us take an example.

T.S. Eliot said that, knowing no Italian, he picked up a copy of Dante and stumbled through a few lines, and knew that this was great poetry. We may attempt the same test with a sonnet of Petrarch's, to see, in reading it aloud, how some of the sound and sense come through. (The reader is warned to notice the triple pun in the first line, and advised that *crine means hair,* and that *leggiadrette* is a diminutive of *charming.*)

> *L'aura che 'l verde lauro e l'aureo crine*
> *soavemente sospirando move,*
> *fa con sue viste leggiadrette e nove*
> *l'anime da' lor corpi pellegrine.*
>   *Candida rosa nata in dure spine,*
> *quando fia chi sua pari al mondo trove?*
> *Gloria di nostra etate! O vivo Giove,*
> *manda, prego, il mio in prima che 'l suo fine;*
>   *sì ch'io non veggia il gran pubblico danno*
> *e 'l mondo remaner senza 'l suo sole,*
> *né li occhi miei, che luce altra non hanno,*
>   *né l'alma, che pensar d'altro non vole,*
> *né l'orecchie, ch'udir altro non sanno*
> *senza l'oneste sue dolci parole.*

What does it mean? Why this:

> *The gentle airs, breathing a little sigh,*
> *lift the green laurel and her golden hair;*
> *and Laura's face, so delicately fair,*

sets free the vagrant soul from body's tie.
*   She is the candid rose, thorn-compassed, shy,*
and yet our age's glory and despair.
O living Jove, grant me this single prayer,
grant only that before her death I die.
*   So I'll not see the sun go out, to bring*
the world's disaster, and to leave behind
my eyes, no other light discovering,
*   my soul, to one unending thought confined,*
my ears, that never hear another thing
but the sweet language of her virtuous mind.

Laura died; and Petrarch commemorated her in his *Triumphs,*
mostly a very exhausting parade before her of ancient heroes and
heroines, in *terza rima.* But there are few sweeter poetic passages
than his description of Laura's death:

*   Non come fiamma che per forza è spenta,*
ma che per sé medesma si consume,
se n'andò in pace l'anima contenta,
*   a guisa d'un soave e chiaro lume*
cui nutrimento a poco a poco manca,
tenendo al fine il suo caro costume.
*   Pallida no, ma più che neve bianca*
che senza venti in un bel colle fiocchi,
parea posar come persona stanca.
*   Quasi un dolce dormir ne' suo' belli occhi,*
sendo lo spirto già da lei diviso,
era quel che morir chiaman gli sciocchi:
*   morte bella parea nel suo bel viso.*

*   Not like a suddenly extinguished light*
her spirit left its earthly tenament.
She dwindled like a flamelet, pure and bright,
*   that lessons in a gradual descent,*
keeping its character while waning low,
spending itself, until its source is spent.
*   Not livid-pale, but whiter than the snow*

the hills in windless weather occupying,
only a mortal languor did she show.
   She closed her eyes; and in sweet slumber lying,
her spirit tiptoed from its lodging-place.
It's folly to shrink in fear, if this is dying;
   for death looked lovely in her lovely face.

This is not, in fact, true; for Laura died of the plague. And any-
way, Petrarch was far away. But what of it?

Petrarch was the first modern scholar, the first modern literary
man (for Dante we must call medieval). He loved to write, rising
often at midnight to get to his desk. A friend tried to force a
vacation on him and locked up his books and papers; Petrarch
fell into feverish headaches, and the friend, alarmed, gave him
back the key.

He wrote, as he read, with passion. He said: "I write to please
myself; and while I write I converse eagerly with our elders, in
one way I can. And I gladly forget those among whom I was
forced by evil fate to live; I employ all my power of mind to escape
them and seek out the ancients. As the very sight of my contemporaries offends me, the remembrance, the splendid deeds,
even the bright names of men of old allure me and fill me with
inestimable joy; so that many would be shocked to learn how
much more I find my delight among the dead than with the
living."

His reading was a communion with ancient spirits, alive in
books. He wrote them personal letters; he called Cicero his father,
Virgil his brother. A great volume of Cicero, disturbed on his
shelves, fell and wounded his ankle, making him wonder what
he had done to make Cicero angry. He called books "welcome,
assiduous companions, always ready to appear in public or go
back in their box at your order, always disposed to speak or be
silent, to stay at home or make a visit to the woods, to travel or
abide in the country, to gossip, joke, encourage you, comfort you,
advise you, reprove you, and take care of you, to teach you the
world's secrets, the records of great deeds, the rules of life and

the scorn of death, moderation in good fortune, fortitude in ill, calmness and constancy in behavior. These are learned, gay, useful, and ready-spoken companions, who will never bring you tedium, expense, lamentation, jealous murmurs, or deception." What a fine quotation for a library, or a publisher!

He served well his ancient friends. He discovered several lost works of Cicero and gave them to his world. With Boccaccio, he engaged an Eastern scholar to translate Homer into Latin. He loved to examine and caress Greek books, though unable to understand them, and he tried in vain to learn the language.

"I have got rid of most of my passions," he wrote a friend, "but I have one insatiable thirst—book-buying." Yet in the end his library numbered only two hundred volumes, partly, to be sure, because he was always giving books away.

We call him the chief reviver of ancient learning. His example stimulated others to collect the classics and to copy them or have them copied. He aroused also a vogue for the critical study of ancient texts, which abounded with copyists' errors. He said that if Cicero or Livy should read current examples of their writing, they would disavow them as the work of barbarians. He developed principles of stylistic analysis, rejecting, on the basis of style alone, works ascribed to Cicero and Virgil. He found a treatise of Saint Ambrose so un-Ambrosian that he took it from the saint and gave it to Palladius.

His own formal Latin style was, and is, recognized as a modern model. It is thoroughly Ciceronian—exact, subtle, sensitive. When a Pope wanted to make him apostolic secretary he escaped the unwanted task by submitting an essay couched in such high style that the Pope rejected it as unpapal. In his letters he employed a lower, familiar manner, easy and flowing, and individual. "The style is the man," he said, long before Buffon. "We all have naturally, as in our person and movements, so in our voice and speech, something singular and our own." He advised a friend not to cling slavishly to the ancients, but to graft the new on the old, for the first inventors were men, too. "Don't believe the common statement that there's nothing new under the sun, and nothing new can be said. True, Solomon and Terence said that; but since their time how much is new!"

His critical sense was keen. He called a treasured document of Julius Caesar a fake; he read an absurd, ill-written life of Saint Simplicianus and said outright that he did not believe a word of it. He opposed supernatural explanations, preferring to rest on plain reason. He was anti-Aristotle, he said, whenever Aristotle was anti-common-sense. He rejected astrology (which was formally taught in Italian universities) because it denied human liberty. "Can celestial bodies deviate from their courses, break all their laws, run in irregular orbits, to give warnings to men? Ridiculous!" He was skeptical even of miracles, since so often lies, follies, and frauds hide under the veil of religion and sanctity.

Essentially, he taught the blending of faith and love with exact, rational, critical method, as he blended in himself the poet and the scholar. One must approach knowledge with emotional desire; one must examine it with cool distrust. "Theology is a poem, with God for subject," he said. But theology is also a rational science, susceptible to reason.

This attitude, this union of love and reason, is humanism. Properly we call Petrarch the first humanist.

With all his modernism, he retained much of the medieval. The word "medieval" would have surprised him; he thought medieval times were modern times, and he thought they were very bad times. He took for granted their social, political, and religious structure, the antithesis of human and divine, the contempt of this world, which is a mere proving ground for the next. But he had no interest in scholastic philosophy or in medieval literature in general. He pinned his faith to Plato, not to Aristotle, the supreme medieval master. While, of course, he knew his immediate poetic predecessors in France and Italy, he never mentions most of the great medieval classics, barely even Dante. He did not own a copy of the *Divine Comedy* until, late in life, he received one as a present from Boccaccio.

He loathed the world that he saw, with a good deal of justifica-

tion, for it was filled with wars, plagues, tyranny, cruelty, ignorance, and political and religious cynicism. He turned backward,
to the Roman classics, to the Bible and the early Fathers, to escape
the present; he dimly realized that his backward-turning was at
the same time a forward-turning.

His times recognized him as an intellectual leader. His fame
was great, first as a poet, then as a moral philosopher. He was
the counselor of princes and of the Emperor, the public critic of
popes. He brought to his age a new concept, or an old, forgotten
concept, of the possibilities of man's existence on earth.

Petrarch was the first man since Saint Augustine, a thousand
years before, to give himself to us entire. His *Letter to Posterity*
is the first modern autobiography. (With a few exceptions, the
Middle Ages barely conceived of the literature of private recollection.) His intense self-consciousness prompted him to self-
analysis, and since he was a literary man, his self-analysis took
shape in self-expression. His enormous collection of letters makes
an endless *journal intime*—and the first.

He was a great introspective. Introspection was hardly a new
discovery. Every religious practiced it, especially the mystics.
However, they were concerned only with the soul's welfare, with
sin and salvation, whereas Petrarch, like any modern, was seeking
first of all self-knowledge. "What use is it to know things if you
don't know yourself?" inquired his mentor, Saint Augustine, in
the *Secretum*. Most of Petrarch's work is an effort to know himself and to display himself completely, with his shortcomings and
faults, and also his virtues. He never tired of exploring his inner
world. We may know him as we know no other man since antiquity, until we come to Montaigne.

We know, as we might have suspected, that his self-consciousness proceeded from a profound youthful self-distrust, *diffidentia*.
To gain confidence and self-mastery, he surrendered to passion
and ambition. But passion and ambition led him far from self-
mastery; it was necessary to subdue them. Finally, recovering
his liberty, he learned to scorn the world, and thus to gain pos-

session of himself and to find at last peace and happiness. His was a lifelong process of self-culture, prompted by and ending in egotism.

His introspection did not prevent him from looking on the external world with delighted, observant eyes. His appreciation of scenic beauty and of country charm has no parallel in medieval literature. His realization of the beauty of mountains was not to reappear in recorded words until the end of the seventeenth century. (He describes, for instance, the blue waters of Como, with the snowy peaks of the Alps overhanging the lake, with forests hiding their heads in clouds, with the dark roaring of torrents pouring out of the heights, and everywhere the murmuring of brooks and the twitter of birds.) He loved flowers and country labors, and when asked his profession liked to reply, "gardener." On the other hand, he did not notice medieval architecture. He mentions only twice, I think, a church's beauty (the golden glitter of St. Mark's in Venice, and the rising Cathedral of Cologne, *pulcherrimum templum.*) The superb Palace of the Popes in Avignon was to him only a gloomy Tartarus. Nor had he much taste for art, though he had Simone Martini paint a small, portable portrait of Laura to sigh over, and though he knew Giotto personally and left in his will one of Giotto's paintings to a friend. ("The ignorant do not understand the beauty of this panel, but the masters of art are stunned by it.") Music, however, he loved; a good concert made him cease to envy the gods their privilege of listening to the music of the spheres.

His sense of beauty awakens occasionally corresponding chords within us. Frequently in his poems, often in his prose, a phrase or set of phrases will leap out as a personal communication over all the years that separate us.

One stormy night in Venice he sat writing late, in his study overlooking the Riva degli Schiavoni. He heard a great shouting below and ran to look down from his highest window. *Deus bone, quod spectaculum!* A number of ships were casting off from the marble quay below. "Their masts considerably overtopped the two corner towers of my palazzo. And at this moment, with all the stars hidden by clouds, as my walls and roofs were shaken by the wind, as the sea roared hellishly below, the ships cast loose from the quay and set forth on their journey. One, perhaps, was bound for the river Don, with passengers for the Ganges, the Caucasus, the Indies, and the Eastern Ocean. My heart bled for these unhappy men. And when I could no longer follow the ships with my eyes, moved and stirred I picked up my pen again, exclaiming: 'Oh, how dear to men is life, and how little account they take of it!' "

Again, he writes: "I had got thus far, and was thinking of what to say next, and as my habit is, I was pricking the paper idly with my pen. And I thought how, between one dip of the pen and the next, time goes on, and I hurry, drive myself, and speed toward death. We are always dying. I while I write, you while you read, and others while they listen or stop their ears, they are all dying."

These are expressions of a modern sensibility, with its awareness of the mystery and marvel of common experience. Petrarch helped to form and define the modern sensibility, which is, indeed, an eternal sensibility. Petrarch is frequently termed the first modern man. I would go farther; I would call him one of the eternal men. As he turned back to find his companions in the great past, we too may turn back, to find in Petrarch a companion and a friend.

II.

Machiavelli

by GARRETT MATTINGLY

For most of us, Renaissance statecraft is typified by a single man, Niccolò Machiavelli—or rather, by a single name, a reputation, an epithet. After all, not many people have any clear recollection of the life and character of the man Machiavelli (not many, even, of the relatively few who have ever bothered to read anything about him). But everyone knows what the name stands for: all the complicated deviltry, hypocrisy, intrigue, secret murders, and public treacheries which for four hundred years the Western world has held typical of the Italian Renaissance. Seventy-five years ago a learned Frenchman identified the whole high Renaissance—the last decades of the fifteenth century and the first ones of the sixteenth—as the Age of Machiavelli. Certainly he realized the incongruity of labeling that bustling time after the drab little servant of a third-rate state, a man whose name even those princes and prelates to whom he had bowed probably never knew or, unless they were Florentines themselves, promptly forgot. But Maulde la Clavière was writing about Renaissance politics, and the name imposed itself. It came as naturally as saying the Age of Augustus, or of Louis le Grand, or of Napoleon, and it carried, like those labels, its own connotations, its own peculiar and, in this case, definitely sinister aura.

In a way it was appropriate that Niccolò Machiavelli should have become the interpreter of Renaissance politics to subsequent ages. He was a Florentine of the Florentines, and the citizens of his city were the quintessence of the new spirit that was then stirring in Italy. Not at first, of course: in the years after the great Guelph victory, after the popes had broken the power of the Empire in Italy forever, Florence was only one of the vigorous, turbulent city republics with which northern and central Italy swarmed. Some of these paid a token allegiance to the Papacy, although the popes knew how little that really meant, and some professed a loyalty to the Holy Roman Emperor, since no Emperor could endanger their liberties any more, but in fact they had all torn clean away from the hierarchical system in which the rest of Christendom was enmeshed, and were engaged in an external struggle against all their neighbors and an internal one of faction against faction, in which the only reality was the naked fact of power.

At first most of these new states were republics. Then, as the bigger fish devoured the smaller, not only were there fewer independent cities, but fewer of the survivors were republics. Presently came the anxious moment when on the Italian mainland only one republic was left, or only one that mattered. By force or guile the great Duke of Milan, Giangaleazzo Visconti, was building himself a kingdom. All Lombardy yielded to him from Piedmont to the Adriatic, and then Genoa and Pisa, Perugia and Siena, and finally proud Bologna. Guarded by its lagoons, the Republic of St. Mark turned its aristocratic back on Italy. Only Florence still held out.

Florence had had as checkered a political history as any of her neighbors. In the century since she had exiled her greatest poet, the bitter factional strife which Dante lamented so pathetically and joined in so energetically had never ceased and only occasionally diminished. In the moment of crisis there was, of course, a clique to say that it would be madness for Florence to pit her unaided strength against the wave of the future, that it would be better for Florentines to live as the subjects of a tyrant then to die as his victims. But the Florentines chose to resist. Apparently they preferred the uneasy vigilance which is the price of freedom to the smug lethargy of the Milanese, and were willing to risk death as free men rather than embrace life as slaves. They did not have to make so hard a choice. As he advanced against Florence, the plague struck down the tyrant, and his jerry-built kingdom fell into ruins. By resisting, the Florentines saved not just their own liberty but the liberties of Italy.

In a series of masterly studies Hans Baron has recently shown how the outcome of this crisis altered the whole tone of Florentine and so of Italian thought. Florence became the center from which spread a new humanism, a new appreciation of political liberty and civic virtue, a new attitude toward the place of man in society. It was this attitude which insured the independence of the major Italian states, and consequently that vigor and diversity of Italian artistic and cultural development which characterized the Renaissance. Now that the point has been made, it seems strange that we did not see it before, but even without Baron's fresh insight, Florentine civic humanism has long been recognized as characteristic of one aspect of the Italian Renaissance. Although he was himself no humanist, if we make that term include a polished mastery of Greek and Latin letters, Niccolò Machiavelli was soaked in the spirit of Florentine humanism.

He was soaked, too, in the Florentine obsession with politics. He came of a family which had played a great role in the political life of his city for more than two centuries. Ancestors of his had been honored, time and again, with the republic's highest offices, and if his father was too stiff-necked a republican to hold a place in a government which was becoming a more and more transparent mask for the boss rule of the Medici, we may be sure that papa Bernardo saw to it that son Niccolò was thoroughly imbued not only with the history of ancient republican Rome, but also with the great traditions of his own city. When he was forty-four, Niccolò wrote that politics was the passion of his life, that he could think and talk of nothing else, and we may guess that this began to be true when he was still young.

For fourteen years he had a chance to indulge his bent in action. When the French invaded Italy in 1494, the Florentines, who had begun to be restive under the scarcely disguised rule of Lorenzo the Magnificent and had become more so under Lorenzo's incompetent son, rose up to reclaim their ancient liberties and drove the Medici out of Florence. Niccolò was then twenty-five. We do not know whether he held any kind of post in the first years of the re-established republic, but when the revolutionary fanatics who were swayed by Savonarola's eloquence gave place to a solider, less hysterical government in 1498, Niccolò Machiavelli, just turned twenty-nine, was appointed second chancellor of the republic. Shortly afterward he was given the additional charge of secretary to the influential committee known as the Dieci di Balia, the Ten of Liberty and Peace as they were sometimes grandiloquently called, or, more realistically, the Ten of War.

War was the chief preoccupation of the restored republic. Foreign armies were tramping back and forth across Italy. Spaniards slowly tightened their grip on Naples; Frenchmen periodically invaded the kingdom and were periodically chased out of Milan; Switzers and Germans were in the field, fighting sometimes for foreign paymasters, sometimes for their own hands; around Rome, first the bastard son of the Borgia Pope and then that warlike old man who succeeded to the Papacy as Julius II were trying to unify the anarchic Papal States; and once all the warring powers put aside their quarrels in order to combine against the one powerful, independent Italian state, the Venetian republic. In the midst of these big wars Florence was busy with an interminable little war, trying to reconquer Pisa, which, in the confusion of the first French invasion, had slipped from under the Florentine yoke. Since his nominal chief, the first chancellor, was more interested in Greek poetry than Italian politics, Machiavelli took a large part in these affairs. He was deep in the business of war and the diplomatic bickerings and hagglings which were the normal Renaissance accompaniments of war. Most of the correspondence of the republic passed through his hands. He wrote memoranda to inform and advise his masters on a variety of subjects, and the Signory sent him on numerous diplomatic missions in Italy, Germany, and France.

Early in his diplomatic career his path crossed that of the man who for most of us typifies the prince of the Age of Machiavelli, the typical prince of the Italian Renaissance—largely because he is the leading figure, the ostensible hero, of Machiavelli's famous little book. Actually, Cesare Borgia was not much more typical of the princes of Italy in his time than Caligula was a typical Roman emperor, or than Al Capone was a typical tax dodger of the age of Herbert Hoover, but there is no denying that for a few years Cesare cut a wide swath and attracted a lot of attention, even eclipsing his notorious father.

Throughout his papacy, the whole family of Rodrigo Borgia, who ascended the papal throne as Alexander VI, was surrounded by a buzz of scandal. Gossiping about popes has always been a favorite Italian pastime, but probably no pope has ever afforded so much occasion for juicy gossip. Other popes had kept mistresses in the Vatican, and simony and immorality were no more rife in Rome under the Borgia Pope than they had been under his predecessors and would be under his successors. But there was a sort of childlike shamelessness about Alexander VI which invited comment. Other popes had auctioned off high ecclesiastical offices, doublecrossed their associates and allies, and used their exalted position for the advancement of their families and for base personal ends, but usually they had pretended that they were doing something else. Rodrigo Borgia had either an honest scorn for hypocrisy or a naïve ignorance of the force of public opinion. Other popes had thrown wild parties at the Vatican, but no other pope had made the parties so flamboyant or so public. And no other pope had had a portrait of his official mistress, robed as the Virgin Mary, painted over the door of his bedchamber or, at the same time, given his official mistress so many transient but reasonably well publicized rivals. Temperate, even ascetic in most respects (in spite, or perhaps because, of his gross body, he drank little wine and ate sparingly of coarse food), Rodrigo Borgia was a great lover of women, and this alone was the source of innumerable stories which grew more outrageous with each retelling.

But neither his private conduct nor his carelessness of concealment can account for all the stories about the Borgia Pope. The trouble was that although far from a saint, he was a first-rate administrator, with enormous energy and a driving will. He tried to police not only the streets of Rome, but even the Roman *campagna,* he tried to control the disorderly Roman nobility, he tried to make sure that the papal treasury received its proper cut of all the sums which the swollen papal bureaucracy and their hangers-on extorted from suitors at his court. He tried, and in part he succeeded, and this made him very unpopular with the Romans. Besides, he tried to assert the rights of the Papacy and his jurisdiction over the Papal States wherever it was challenged, whether by the Duke of Milan or the republics of Venice or Florence, by the King of Naples or the anarchic Neapolitan barons, or by the petty tyrants of Umbria and the Romagna. This made him unpopular with the ruling classes throughout Italy. Worst of all, he was a foreigner, a Spaniard, and Italians have always resented a non-Italian pope. Hence another whole cluster of stories, different and more sinister.

Two of Rodrigo Borgia's children, his eldest son, the Duke of Gandia, and his daughter Lucrezia, were less than ideal targets for malicious gossip. Gandia, although he inherited to some extent his father's disposition to run after women, was otherwise a conventional and colorless type. Lucrezia, although she had a checkered and somewhat smirched history of successive marriages before she was out of her teens—a foundation on which Roman scandalmongers readily erected a towering superstructure—was really a bland, vapid creature with nothing remarkable about her except a cowlike disposition and long blonde hair. But the Pope's younger son, Cesare, was something else again. Even as a mere stripling, just turned seventeen and newly made a cardinal, he was already a spectacular figure, taller by a head than most tall men, with massive shoulders, a wasp waist, classically regular features, a leonine mane, and blazing blue eyes. It was said that he could leap into the saddle wthout touching pommel or stirrups, bend a silver *scudo* double between his fingers, or straighten the iron of a horseshoe with a twist of his wrist. And he was a show-off. He dressed himself and his household with insolent magnificence, and he used to organize *corridas* in the Piazza Navona so that the Romans could watch him behead a bull with a single stroke of a broadsword. Before long he was trailing a legend gaudier and more lurid than that attached to his father.

It was said that he was his father's rival for his sister's incestuous bed. (Almost certainly false.) It was said that after the horrible sack of Capua he seized forty beautiful highborn maidens and added them to his personal harem. (Highly unlikely. Cesare does not seem to have shared his father's excessive appetite. The maidens were probably commandeered by Cesare's captains, though perhaps in his name.) It was said that he seduced that gallant youth Astorre Manfredi, and when he tired of him had him murdered. (Possible, but the motive for the murder was more probably purely political.) It was said that he had murdered his brother, the Duke of Gandia. (Probable. At least his father seems to have believed it.) And that he had his brother-in-law, Lucrezia's second husband, murdered. (Pretty certainly true.) But it was a dull week when one, at least, of the embassies in Rome did not chalk up another murder to Cesare's credit, sometimes by poison, sometimes by the hands of hired assassins, sometimes by his own dagger. Probably he really was responsible for a fair share of those bodies hauled out of the Tiber. Freed by his brother's death from his cardinalate, Cesare became Duke de Valentinois (Valentino, the Italians called him) and Gonfaloniere of the Church, cousin and ally of the King of France, and commander in chief of the papal army. As he marched through the anarchic Papal States, seizing one town after another, by bribery or trickery or the sheer terror of his name, his legend hung over him like a thundercloud.

When Machiavelli first encountered the Duke, the spell of the legend must have been already at work on him, and it must have been heightened by the manner in which Valentino received him and his chief, at night, by the light of a single flickering candle which showed only dimly the tall figure clad in black from head to foot without jewel or ornament, the still white features as regular as a Greek statue and as immobile. Perhaps the cold beauty of those marble features was already beginning to be marred by the pustules which led Valentino later on usually to wear a mask. Perhaps the eyes, lost in shadow, already held that glare which another ambassador noted in them shortly afterward, the look of a savage beast at bay. And perhaps a shrewder observer might have reflected that there was the smell of comedy about these negotiations, the Duke endlessly repeating the same banalities about his eternal friendship for Florence and how wise the republic would be to employ the services of so good a friend, while his captains warned the Florentine envoys that the Duke's patience was growing short, that France would support him against Florence and the Venetians would not stir, that the army was poised to spring and could be at the city's gates before the news of its coming. It was really one of the cruder forms of blackmail, but something about the Duke's personality put the act over, and the Florentine envoys carried away the image of a great prince, subtle, inscrutable, dangerous.

Not long afterward Machiavelli had an opportunity to observe Cesare Borgia in action at the time of his greatest triumph. Cesare was not much of a general: he never learned the rudiments of tactics or strategy, logistics or supply. He was not even a good combat leader, and though he has been praised as a disciplinarian, the only available instance seems to be that once he quelled an incipient riot among some of his brawling soldiers by the terror of his presence. Similarly, if he ever gave any proof of ability as a statesman or ruler, no evidence survives. But he was a ruthless gangster and an expert confidence man, and the revolt of some of the smaller gangsters, his captains, gave him an opportunity to display his talents. Machiavelli watched, fascinated, while Cesare, all mildness and good will, lured his mutinous subordinates into a peace conference, lulled their fears, invited them to a banquet to celebrate their renewed friendship, and when they arrived unarmed and unescorted at a rendezvous where Cesare had hidden his bodyguards, had them seized and murdered. Machiavelli was delighted at the virtuosity of the performance and set it all down in detail for the edification of his countrymen and of posterity.

Machiavelli had a third opportunity to observe the Duke. He arrived in Rome on the business of the republic some months after the death of Alexander VI and just at the moment when Cesare, with incredible stupidity, had helped swing the election of his most implacable enemy. It was plain to see that Cesare was finished. Everything really had depended on his father's being Pope, and as soon as his father died, his allies deserted him, his people rose against him, and his army fell apart as his captains scrambled for the service of some luckier master. Machiavelli assessed the emptiness of the man at a glance, avoided him when he could, wrote of him and no doubt looked at him with cold contempt. But later Machiavelli seems to have preferred to forget the cringing, whimpering, blustering, dithering creature his hero had become. The picture is spread out in detail in his dispatches, but Machiavelli never openly alluded to this aspect of Cesare again.

One thing Machiavelli admired about Cesare was that he raised his soldiers in his own domain instead of hiring foreign mercenaries. It was not, in fact, a great departure. The Romagna was the great source of mercenary troops, and for years its petty despots had enrolled their subjects and farmed them out to fight other people's wars. But Cesare's action was like a project very close to Machiavelli's heart, one which after years of urging he finally got the Florentine government to adopt. They not only adopted it, they put him in charge of it, so that for the last six years of the republic he had added to his other duties most of those of minister of defense. Instead of the cut-rate mercenaries who had prolonged the Pisan war for twelve years (being a republic in which the taxpayers held the purse strings, Florence hired only the cheapest mercenaries), Machiavelli persuaded the government to raise a militia in its own territory. Since the militia were not Florentine citizens, but conscripts from the wretched peasants of the *contado,* a folk without political rights or any material stake in the success of their bourgeois masters, the scheme had an obvious weakness, but it did not work badly at first. In 1509 Pisa fell, and Machiavelli's militia could claim a share in the long-delayed triumph. Three years later the militia failed a harder test. When the veteran Spanish infantry moved in to attack Prato, the militia ran like rabbits, and the Medici epigoni came back behind a column of Spanish pikes to rule once more in Florence. Machiavelli's active career in politics was over. But not his interest in politics. The next year he wrote that he could think about, talk about, nothing else, and from then on until he died in 1527, only a few weeks after the Florentines had again expelled the Medici, most of the writings with which he sought to allay the boredom of his exclusion from office were concerned, one way and another, with statecraft. He also wrote some verses—pretty wretched verses—and a not unamusing version of an old, smutty joke, and comedies, one of which is a masterpiece. But mostly he wrote about politics. Had he been asked to name his political writings in an ascending order of importance, surely the top three would have been his *History of Florence,* his *Art of War*, and his *Discourses on the First Ten Books of Livy.* Into these writings, and particularly into the last, Machiavelli had poured, or so he thought, all his practical experience of government and diplomacy and all his wide reading of ancient and modern history. However surprised some of the successful statesmen of his day might have been to find the little Florentine secretary the political spokesman of their age, Machiavelli himself would not have been too surprised. He would have regarded the reputation accrued as a poor compensation for the fame as a statesman which fate had denied him, but he had often said that he was the first modern man to look at politics with a clear and open eye, and he would certainly have taken the recognition of posterity as no more than due to the merit of his books.

Only, of course, the recognition of posterity has nothing to do with the books Machiavelli would have named. When people speak of the Age of Machiavelli, they are not thinking of any of them, but of one little pamphlet apparently dashed off at white heat in 1513 just after the fall of the Florentine republic. It is called *The Prince* and it bears only an ambiguous, tangential relationship to Machiavelli's big, serious works or, some people think, to the actual history of the time and place over which its fame casts such a lurid and sinister light. The discrepancy between the impression of Renaissance Italy to be gathered from *The Prince* and that given by the rest of Machiavelli's writings, to say nothing of the writings of his contemporaries, who often turn out to be more reliable about matters of fact, is sufficient to raise some doubts about the appropriateness of letting *The Prince* describe the political atmosphere of its time.

Perhaps our doubts about letting Machiavelli speak for the age which bears his name ought not to be increased by our knowledge of his private life. But among his contemporaries, surely Niccolò Machiavelli was one of the least Machiavellian. It is true that he often professed a preference for drastic methods and for sweeping all-or-nothing solutions, along with a contempt for delay and improvisation and compromise, a set of attitudes usually more characteristic of academic theorists than of practical men of affairs. But though this quirk of temperament sometimes misled him into a temporary enthusiasm for a mountebank like Cesare Borgia, it does not seem otherwise to have affected his own behavior. If the discipline of the Florentine militia had been harsher, they might not have run so soon at Prato. Machiavelli not seldom praised the efficacy of hypocrisy and smooth deceit, but in his dealings both with his own government and with foreign potentates, he was usually inept at concealing his feelings, likely to show his hand, and, in negotiation, blunt to the point of tactlessness. He often spoke of the value of clear-eyed, dispassionate observation and seems rather to have prided himself on the possession of this faculty, but, in fact, his views were usually clouded by wish and prejudice, he was easily deceived, and he was not, in the things that really mattered, those affecting the daily course of politics, a very acute, discriminating, or even very accurate observer. This judgment, suggested by comparing his dispatches with those of his contemporaries, is reinforced by the fact that his employers, the Florentine Signory, never gave him the chief responsibility for any important mission.

Niccolò not only lacked the virtues he praised, he possessed others even more incompatible with our picture of Old Nick. He was as anticlerical as most literate adult male Italians of the last six centuries have always been, and, in spite of his pious mother's teaching, no more zealously practicing a Catholic than one would expect. But as he had been baptized, confirmed, and married, so he died in the arms of the Church, having seen to it that his children followed the same conventional course. Nor—and this is farther from the popular picture of his age—is there any evidence that he indulged in any fantastic crimes or vices. He was probably no more faithful to his wife than most middle-class husbands in any age or clime, but he seems to have been a kind, affectionate considerate husband and father, as he was a warm and true friend, a man of his word in money matters, and an admired and respected citizen.

A digression may be called for here about the handful of pornographic letters which shocked the Victorian sensibilities of J. A. Symonds. The fifteenth-century humanists had made fantastic obscenities a normal epistolary ornament. Certainly no Anglo-Saxon in the last two centuries would have written down such anecdotes about himself as Machiavelli wrote to his friends, though they are not much different from what one may hear in any locker room or thoroughly masculine bar. But they are responses, all of them, to anecdotes which his friends wrote him, and they differ from them not in essential subject matter but in elaboration and intensification. They are clearly meant to top his friends' stories, and do top them so successfully that one is led to wonder whether literary artifice and imagination have not been called in to supply the defects of experience. Machiavelli, himself, would have been the first to resent the implication that he was a saint. But there is not the slightest evidence that he was anything but the most conventional, commonplace, and prudent kind of sinner.

One inappropriate virtue is particularly surprising. It even surprised Machiavelli himself. The man who wrote that men are moved so predominantly by self-interest that princes need take account of no other motives, that "a man will resent the loss of his

patrimony more than the murder of his father," was himself the
devoted, unselfish servant of his ungrateful state. He lived in an
age when the use of public office for private gain was perfectly
customary. He had during most of his fourteen years as a servant
of the Florentine republic unrivaled opportunities to enrich himself at the expense of the condottieri and other contractors with
whom as secretary to the Ten of War he had to deal. Yet he
quitted the Florentine service as poor as the day he had entered
it. His whole public career was a testimony to the inaccuracy of
his own cynical maxims. It is hard to reconcile it with the trend
of his major serious books. It is impossible to square it with the
lurid picture which we have drawn from his one famous little
book, *The Prince*.

Drawn, in part, quite unjustifiably. Most people, whether they
have read *The Prince* or not, retain the conviction that somewhere,
they cannot say quite where, Machiavelli commends the famous
(quite mythical) poison of the Borgia and justifies the pagan
debauchery which, ever since the Reformation, Protestant countries have associated with the Italian Renaissance.

Most of these false imputations are quite old and go back to a
book called *Anti-Machiavel* which a Huguenot pamphleteer wrote
against Catherine de' Medici and her Italian entourage just after
the Massacre of St. Bartholomew's. But even after these old vulgar
errors have been cleared out of the way, *The Prince* remains a
shocking book, shocking both for what it says and for the deliberately provocative way it says it, and for the discord between a part
of its contents and the life and other writings of its author.

As for its contents: *The Prince* lays it down as a major premise
that men in general are selfish, treacherous, cowardly, greedy,
and, above all, gullible and stupid. It therefore advises a prince,
and particularly a new prince who hopes to destroy the liberties
of those he rules, to employ hypocrisy, cruelty, and deceit, to
make himself feared even at the risk of making himself hated, to
divide the people and destroy their natural leaders, and to keep
faith with no one, since no one will keep faith with him. It views
the world of politics as a jungle in which moral laws and standards

of ethical conduct are merely snares for fools, a jungle in which there is no reality but power, and power is the reward of ruthlessness, ferocity, and cunning. In such a jungle, not the actual Cesare Borgia, but the picture of himself which Cesare succeeded in conveying at the height of his fame, a savage beast—half lion and half fox—would be the natural king. To a society which regarded the relations between its parts as ruled by justice and equity and sanctified by religion, all this was more shocking than we can quite imagine.

It was shocking, too, to find a man of staunch republican principles and flawless republican antecedents, a man who had served the Florentine republic with selfless devotion and suffered for that devotion more than most, turning, within months of his country's fall, to writing a handbook for tyrants, a book meant to teach the Medici, the enemies of his country's liberties, how to hold his fellow countrymen in thrall, and writing it all for the mean object of helping himself to wriggle back into some minor government post. If Machiavelli behaved so, he earned, for the only time in his life, the epithet Machiavellian. That his behavior seems to have been a momentary aberration, that when it was over Machiavelli returned to the defense of republican principles and the society of republican friends, makes his defection not less shocking but only more puzzling.

From the first there were at least two explanations of the puzzle. One was that Machiavelli had been inspired by the Evil One to write a plausible book of advice for princes, meant to damn the souls and ruin the fortunes of princes who followed it, and to destroy the prosperity of their subjects. This was the official view, shared by the cardinals and popes who placed and kept *The Prince* on the Index and by the Protestant pamphleteers who pointed to it as the manual of the Jesuits and the political inspiration of the Counter Reformation. Meanwhile a second view was expressed openly by some of Machiavelli's fellow countrymen (those in exile) and hinted at by some who remained in Italy, where the banned book continued clandestinely to circulate. This was that *The Prince,* under the guise of giving advice to princes,

was meant to warn all free men of the dangers of tyranny. One
wonders whether the originators of this explanation of the puzzle
may not have been the ardent Florentine republicans who always
remained Machiavelli's friends. From this second view sprang the
judgment, popular in the eighteenth century, that *The Prince* was,
in fact, a satire on absolute monarchy, and that all its epigrams
were deliberately double-edged. The nineteenth century offered
other solutions to the puzzle. The one which gained ascendancy
as the cause of national self-determination triumphed in Western
Europe was that, ardent republican though he was, Machiavelli
made up his mind that only a strong prince could liberate Italy
from the barbarians, and so chose to sacrifice the freedom of
his city to the unity of Italy. Just before World War I, this solution
began to be questioned by those who said that Machiavelli was
not a chauvinistic patriot but a detached, dispassionate political
scientist who described political behavior as it actually was. After
about 1920 this view took a powerful lead over all its competitors,
and among orthodox Machiavelli scholars it still dominates the
field.

Obviously none of these answers is entirely satisfactory. It is
possible that Machiavelli was mean enough to sell his birthright
of republican ideals for the chance of some third-rate civil service
post under a petty tyrant; but that he was at the same time stupid
enough to believe that a book like *The Prince* was the best way
into Medici favor, and to let advice which, if it was seriously
meant, should have been highly secret escape into general circula-
tion, seems much less credible. Both the notion that *The Prince*
was inspired by the devil and the counternotion that it was the
subtle weapon of republican idealism seem equally oversimplified.
And, of course, the proposal that *The Prince* was conceived as a
satire is the kind of anachronism which only the eighteenth century
could have perpetrated. Machiavelli knew perfectly well that sat-
ires were compositions in verse after the manner of Horace and
Juvenal, such as his friend Luigi Alamanni wrote. He would have
failed completely to understand the proposition that *The Prince*
was a satire. As for the theory that Machiavelli was willing to

accept a tyrant prince in order to effect the unification of Italy, there is not the faintest indication anywhere in his writings that he would have grasped the idea if anybody had put it to him. There is nothing about unifying Italy anywhere in *The Prince,* only about driving out the barbarians, a commonplace of Italian rhetoric from Petrarch to Paul IV. But Machiavelli the Italian patriot is a little easier to swallow than Machiavelli the dispassionate scientist, unless someone can explain how the scientific temper can accord with facts and generalizations equally distorted by emotion and prejudice.

It is probably hopeless to try to explain the whole puzzle of *The Prince.* How do you reconstruct the motives at a particular moment of a man more than four hundred years in his grave who has left only the scantiest and most ambiguous clues to what they might be? How do you tell, in the case of a man like Machiavelli, how much of the demonstrable distortion in *The Prince* was due to faulty observation (he was a passionate man), and how much to the deliberate irony which he certainly sometimes practiced? How do you probe the bitterness and agony of spirit which must certainly have been his on the collapse of all his hopes, and decide which wild statements come from anger, which from despair, and which from a calculated will to undermine his enemies by indirection?

Probably, like most insoluble problems about men of genius, this one has taken up more time and energy than it deserves. The real importance of Machiavelli, his claim to give his name to a whole period of history, lies elsewhere, not in the points in which *The Prince* differs from his other writings, but in those in which it agrees. Here the transformation of his legendary figure from a diabolist or a rebel, a spirit who says "No," to a major culture hero, offers the clue. What had happened, in almost three centuries between the time when Machiavelli was either praised as a daring rebel or denounced as an emissary of Satan and the time when he began to be acclaimed as a prophet, was that all Europe had become what Italy in Machiavelli's lifetime already was, a congeries of autonomous, purely temporal sovereign states, without any common end to bind them into a single society or any interest higher than their own egotistical drives for survival and expansion.

To pretend that the relations between such states were governed by Christian ethics seemed to Machiavelli a contemptible hypocrisy. Many Italians since Dante had lamented that the nearer one came to Rome the wider the gap between Christian teaching and Christian practice, and charged that the Papacy had corrupted the morals of Italy. Indeed, the major assumption of the stern reformers of what we call the Counter Reformation was not much different. But Machiavelli went further. He compared his own embittered picture of the degeneracy of his countrymen with Livy's of the virtues of republican Rome, and without asking how much exaggeration there might be in either, he leaped to one of his drastic all-or-nothing conclusions. Christianity, whatever its value as a guide in private life, was not a viable fountain for the good society. So for the religion of Christ he proposed to substitute the religion of patriotism. In politics the Christian ethic was worse than valueless, it was positively harmful. It might serve to keep the masses more law-abiding in their private lives, but when it came to public actions the only test of good or bad was what best served the safety and aggrandizement of the state. Since every state was an autonomous entity, recognizing no superior and no interest higher than its own, no rules of ethics whatever applied to relations between states. The only test was success. This was Machiavelli's consistent position. It appears in his earliest state papers and is as firmly held in his writings in praise of republics as it is in *The Prince*. In 1513 it was a desperate paradox. By 1813 it was an axiom of statecraft. By 1914 it was the tritest of platitudes. Machiavelli did not invent it. It was apparent in the behavior of the Italian states of his time and more or less openly acknowledged in the memoranda of statesmen and diplomats. But Niccolò Machiavelli first gave the fresh attitude of his age toward statecraft a permanent literary form, and the progress of history compelled general recognition of his insight. For that reason, perhaps he does deserve to be accepted as the voice of the Renaissance State. Perhaps his age should be called "The Age of Machiavelli."

III.

The Young Michelangelo

by KENNETH CLARK

Michelangelo belongs to that small company of poets, artists, and musicians whose greatness has never been seriously questioned; but he differs from his companions—Dante, Shakespeare, Goethe, Titian, Mozart—in one important way. All of them have maintained this hold on our admiration by appealing to a wide range of human experience, so that each generation may extract from their works what suits it best. But Michelangelo has made his own terms with posterity, just as he did with his employers. He is the most concentrated and undeviating of great artists. We come to him for one particular revelation, communicated by one particular means. And the revelation is so important to us, and the mastery of means so absolute, that having once experienced it we, like his contemporaries, can never get it out of our systems. It makes everything else seem small and tame and worldly.

When we speak of an artist's greatness, as opposed to his talent or even his genius, we are usually referring to an aspect of his personality, and this is particularly true of Michelangelo. We know about him from many contemporary records, including the two *Lives* of Condivi and Vasari, men who knew him well, and every one of these records gives us the impression of an awe-inspiring character. Leaving aside the great religious teachers, I cannot think of any other man in history who has commanded such respect.

Our visual image of Michelangelo is of an old man, his face deeply marked by spiritual struggles. But there is a quantity of evidence that as a young man his force of character was equally apparent. The following episode recorded by Condivi will serve as an example. In 1506 Michelangelo had left Rome in a huff because he had been debarred from immediate access to Pope Julius II. Seven months later Michelangelo was brought into the papal presence. Julius asked him why he had walked out. Michelangelo answered, "Not from ill will, but from disdain" (*ma per isdegno*). A bishop who was present nervously intervened, "Pay no attention, Your Holiness; he speaks out of ignorance. Artists are all like that." But before the wretched bishop could finish his apology he was hustled out of the room with blows; and Michelangelo resumed his former relationship with the Pope. Julius was then the most formidable figure in Christendom; Michelangelo was thirty-two.

Michelangelo used this transcendent force of character, which was like the spiritual power of a medieval saint, to transform the physical perfection of antiquity. He appeared at the moment when Greco-Roman sculpture was a new and compelling discovery, accepted by artists and patrons alike as an ultimate model. But in fact the bland materialism of antique art could not alone have expressed the crisis of the human spirit which took place during the years between Luther and Galileo. Michelangelo, by changing and twisting the forms of antique sculpture, created an instrument through which the spiritual turmoil of the sixteenth century could be made visible.

He was born in Florentine territory on March 6, 1475, and was one of the very few artists to come of aristocratic stock, although by his time the family fortunes had declined. His father, who claimed descent from the counts of Canossa, strongly objected to his son becoming an artist, which at that date meant an artisan; and when Michelangelo was one of the most famous men in Italy, his father still regarded the whole affair with bewildered incredulity. He was, as Convidi says, "somewhat old-fashioned"; but Michelangelo treated him with patience and respect, asked for his prayers and sent him money, and often said that his sole aim in life had been to help the family regain its former status.

From the very first no one had any doubt that he was supremely gifted in the arts of design. After a short apprenticeship with Ghirlandaio, the most successful Florentine painter of the period, he is said by his biographers to have joined the privileged youths who were drawing antiques in the Medici gardens of the Via Larga, under the direction of the sculptor Bertoldo, and where he attracted the attention of Lorenzo the Magnificent. I see no adequate reason for disbelieving this tradition, and Michelangelo's earliest carvings seem to confirm it, for they consist largely of imitations of the antique, of a kind which he would have learned only in this particular school. Bertoldo's own masterpiece was a bronze relief of a battle, done in imitation of an antique sarcophagus in Pisa; and Michelangelo's earliest carving is also an imitation of a battle sarcophagus, although the nominal subject is the *Rape of Dejanira.* Although it was surely begun in the Medicean academy (and was perhaps left unfinished on Lorenzo's death in 1492) it looks out of this enchanted garden, both backwards and forwards: back to the charged and passionate Last Judgments of the Pisani and forward to the achievements of Michelangelo's maturity. There is no more striking example of Proust's saying, *"Les grands artistes n'ont jamais fait qu'une seule oeuvre."* Michelangelo's first great carving foreshadows not only the classical style of his Florentine period, but the anticlassical expressiveness of his later works. In many respects it is closer to the *Last Judgment* of the Sistine than to the cartoon of the *Battle of Cascina.* And the affinity with the Dantesque spirit of Giovanni Pisano is also very revealing, for Michelangelo's heroic seriousness was, perhaps unconsciously, a reaction away from the daintiness of the *quattrocento,* back to the passion and gravity of the first founders of Tuscan art. His earliest drawings were copies of Giotto, and the poems of Dante were his continual inspiration.

But the Dejanira relief is exceptional. During his years in the garden of the Via Larga, and for some time afterward, Michelangelo's whole conscious effort was directed toward the imitation of the classical style, and he succeeded so well that one of his works, a sleeping cupid, was actually sold as an antique, having been buried in a vineyard by a Roman dealer. When the fraud was discovered, Michelangelo, unlike modern imitators of antiquity, derived nothing but credit for his skill, and the cupid was afterwards purchased by that most pedantic of collectors, Isabella d'Este. It has now disappeared, and the *Bacchus,* which survives from about the same epoch, suggests that the loss is not a serious one. For the *Bacchus* is an all too successful imitation of Hellenistic sculpture at its least attractive. The swaying, dreamy movement of the body and a certain Dionysiac beauty in the head do not compensate for the lack of tension in the modeling, and one is left wondering how Michelangelo, even in a technical exercise, has contrived to suppress his energy of hand.

The *Bacchus* was executed in Rome, soon after Michelangelo's arrival there in 1496. After the death of Lorenzo de' Medici in 1492 he had remained two years in Florence, and it was at this time that he is supposed to have begun a scientific study of anatomy, under the protection of the Prior of Santo Spirito. These were the years when Savonarola was the virtual ruler of Florence, and although Michelangelo was never a direct follower, he read Savonarola's books throughout his life, and told Condivi that he could still hear the *frate*'s voice ringing in his ears. So two essential ingredients of Michelangelo's art, a passion for anatomy and a consciousness of sin, were, so to say, poured into his mind at the same moment. But he was not happy in the Florence of Piero de' Medici; and in October, 1494, there occurred the first of those panic flights which were to be repeated three times in the course of his life. Psychologists have occupied themselves with the question why this man of immense moral courage, who was utterly indifferent to physical hardship, should have suffered from these recurrences of irrational fear; and perhaps it is true that continuous inner tension led to an occasional snapping of the spirit, which expressed itself in a sudden need to escape. Or perhaps in each case there really was some ground for running away, and Michelangelo, who recognized his own genius, felt that he must preserve his life at any cost. In 1494 he fled to Bologna, where, as usual, his gifts were immediately recognized and he was commissioned to work on the chief sculptural project of the town, the ark of Saint Dominic; but fifteenth-century Bologna offered no scope to a youth of Michelangelo's genius, and as soon as possible he returned to Florence, and thence to Rome.

He arrived in Rome in the summer of 1496, having a letter of introduction from Lorenzo di Pierfrancesco de' Medici, the pupil of Marsilio Ficino and friend of Botticelli; and a week after his arrival he wrote back to Lorenzo, "There are many beautiful things here." Medieval Rome, the city of vineyards and cow pastures, with its stranded basilicas and aggressive watchtowers, was just beginning to give up its buried treasure; and Michelangelo's chief patron at this epoch, Jacopo Galli, had already a considerable collection of antiques, amongst which Michelangelo's *Bacchus* was given a place of honor. However, the outstanding work during this first visit to Rome was of an entirely different character, the *Pietà* in St. Peter's. It was commissioned by a French cardinal, Jean Bilheres, and this may account for the fact that Michelangelo accepted a Gothic motif in which the full-grown Christ lies on Our Lady's knees. This was originally a wood-carving motif, and the difficulty of adapting it to the crystalline character of marble has led Michelangelo to a marvelous feat of technical skill. This is the first work in which he shows that consummate mastery of his craft which his contemporaries, both artists and patrons, valued so highly. It has also involved a new stretch of the imagination, for he has achieved what theorists tell us is impossible, a perfect fusion of Gothic and Classic art. The motif and sentiment are northern, the physical beauty of the nude Christ is Greek; and Michelangelo has given the Virgin's head, so painfully distorted in Gothic Pietàs, a union of physical and spiritual beauty which is entirely his own. Ever since the *Pietà* was put in place, people have asked how the mother of a grown man, in the depths of grief, could appear so young and beautiful; and Michelangelo's reply is recorded in both Vassari and Condivi. It expresses in vivid, colloquial form the doctrines of Neoplatonism, which he had absorbed from the Medicean philosophers of his boyhood: that physical perfection is the mirror and emblem of a pure and noble spirit. This is the belief that had led his friend Lorenzo di Pierfrancesco to commission Botticello's *Venus;* and we know, from Michelangelo's sonnets, that it justified to his mind his passionate admiration of the naked beauty of young men. Our scientific modern way of thinking, with its reliance on experience and psychology, may reject Neoplatonism as a compound of myth and self-deception. But there is no question of the sincerity with which Michelangelo believed (in Spenser's words) that "soule is form, and doth the bodie make."

In 1501 Michelangelo returned to Florence. These were the years in which the Florentine republic was able to assert some of the heroic virtues which had made it great a century before, and Michelangelo must have found the atmosphere of his native city a sharp contrast to the Medicean *douceur de vivre* of his youth, or the parasitic, antiquarian Rome of his more recent experience. It was an atmosphere which suited him perfectly, and he was immediately called upon by the city magistrates to carry out commissions which should express the pride, vigor, and austere idealism of their regime; and the results were the *David* and the cartoon of the *Battle of Cascina.*

The *David* was carved out of a gigantic block of marble from which, seventy years earlier, the sculptor Agostino di Duccio had begun to carve the figure of a prophet. Agostino had completed little more than a knot of drapery, and when at last the derelict block was given to Michelangelo, his first symbolic act was to cut this drapery away. In his austere and uncompromising nudity the *David* states for the first time the essence of Michelangelo's ideal. As a piece of modeling the torso is equal to the finest work of antiquity, both in science and plastic vitality. Cut out the head and the hands, and you have one of the most perfect classical works of the Renaissance. Put them back and you put back the rough Tuscan accent, which was part of his birthright. It is possible to feel that there is a certain lack of harmony between the two elements: the *David* is in many respects an imperfect work. The marble block was too thin, and apart from this material shortcoming, Michelangelo has made a mistake common at the time; he has taken a motif from a relief as the basis for a figure in the round. But if the whole is unsatisfactory, the *David,* taken part by part, is a work of overwhelming power and magnificence, and it is Michelangelo's first great assertion of that quality which is so often in our minds when we think of him—the heroic. I suppose that the heroic in life or art is based on the consciousness that life is a struggle; and that in this struggle it is courage, strength of will, and determination which are decisive, not intelligence nor sensibility. The heroic involves a contempt of convenience and a sacrifice of all those pleasures which contribute to what we call a civilized life. It is the enemy of happiness. But we recognize that it is man's supreme achievement. For the heroic is not merely a struggle with material obstacles; it is a struggle with Fate. Insofar as it magnifies the individual in his conflict with the blind forces of destiny it is the highest expression of a humanist ideal, and was recognized as such in antiquity. But the heroic stands on the borders of humanism, and looks beyond it. For to struggle with Fate man must become more than man; he must aspire to be a god. Now apotheosis announced the end of human art. If there is a single point at which the art of classical antiquity turns toward the Middle Ages, it is when the emperor is accepted as a god. The first great medieval work of art is the statue of Constantine at Barletta: and like the *David* it is of heroic size. So on the perfectly antique body of the *David* is set a head which looks, with proud and conscious heroism, away from the happy, concrete world of the *quattrocento.* Like other great revolutions in history, we may wish that it had never happened, but once it has taken place we must accept it with all its potency for good or evil.

The mere size of the *David* (the statue stands over sixteen feet high), which is embarrassing to us, impressed Michelangelo's contemporaries. As a technical achievement alone it was a source of civic pride, like a space rocket. Significantly, the committee of artists who considered its site took it away from the cathedral and placed it in front of the Palazzo della Signoria, the center of democratic government. A few months later Michelangelo began, in this building, the other great composition of these heroic Florentine years, the *Battle of Cascina*. It was executed in rivalry with Leonardo da Vinci, but unlike his *Battle of Anghiari,* it was never carried out as a painting, and the cartoon on which it was drawn proved so irresistible to artists that it was soon cut up and lost. Vasari called it "the school of all the world," and Benvenuto Cellini was certainly voicing the professional verdict when he said that Michelangelo never did better. What gave it this immense authority? We can see from copies and from Michelangelo's original studies that it consisted of a number of naked men grouped in such a way as to show off the human body in action. Each body was not only an admirable human specimen modeled with scientific knowledge, but was in a pose selected for its completeness and nobility. Such poses were the legacy of antique art, surviving almost like symbols, through four hundred years of attrition; and in fact some of Michelangelo's drawings for the *Battle* are not done from nature, but from wax models he had made of antiques. So the *Battle of Casina* was the foundation of the academic ideal, that strange, compelling approach to form which dominated art education until the present century; and the fact that Michelangelo himself transcended this ideal has always been a source of confusion to his more academic admirers.

For Michelangelo's vision of antique art was not bounded by the firm and finished outlines of the Cascina drawings. Throughout his life he had two ideals of antiquity which were in a sense complementary to each other. One of these was the ideal of perfection, the belief that what gave antique art its durability was the unflinching firmness with which every detail was realized. This had inspired the *Bacchus* and the *David*, and was to be realized, in later life, in those curious labors of love, the drawings executed for his friend Tomasso de' Cavalieri. For these the source of his inspiration was chiefly cameos and gems. But parallel with this admiration for its completeness, Michelangelo was fascinated by the fragmentary character of ancient sculpture; and the appeal of these weather-worn survivors of a mightier age was all the stronger because they gave a free play to the imagination. This attitude to ruins and fragments became common in what we call the Romantic Movement. Michelangelo was not the first man to feel it—Mantegna had already made evocative use of ruins—but he was the first to let it influence his style. Like the half lines in Virgil, the rough and unfinished state of Michelangelo's sculpture has evoked a whole literature of explanation, and no doubt the cause lies deep in his temperament. But I am certain that he was encouraged in this means of expression by the suggestive decay of antique sculpture. A proof of this dates from the very period of the *Battle* cartoon, the unfinished figure of Saint Matthew, commissioned by the Duomo in 1503 and executed a year or two later. It is imitated from a battered Roman figure, the so-called *Pasquino,* which had already inspired Donatello; and I doubt if this rather grotesque work would have had so compelling an appeal to the imagination of two great artists had it been better preserved. In decay only the large lines of movement were perceptible, and gave the effect of a giant struggling out of the mists of antiquity.

This sense of titanic struggle was an aspect of Michelangelo's character which had appeared already in the Dejanira relief, and came more and more to dominate his art; and the crumbling magnificence of antique sculpture showed him that he could express it by leaving a great deal to the spectator's imagination. This also involved two other advantages which, although not consonant with the artistic principles of Michelangelo's time, appeal most strongly to our own: it allowed him to preserve the character of his material with the vivid mark of his own hand upon it; and it allowed him to dispense with those parts of a figure which did not fit into the main rhythm of his design, just as time has lopped off such excrescences as the arms of the *Torso Belvedere.*

This titanic struggle of form to emerge from matter reaches its climax in the marble figures destined for the tomb of Julius II. Michelangelo had been summoned to Rome in March, 1505, and commanded to design and execute the greatest tomb in Christendom. His new master was a formidable man of action, with a powerful mind and boundless ambition. He was also as proud and willful as Michelangelo himself. Gorki once said of Tolstoy, "His relations with God are very uneasy: like two old bears in a den," and such were Michelangelo's relations with God's vicar on earth. Yet it was one of those momentous conjunctions for which posterity must be grateful, for without Julius II, Michelangelo might never have had the opportunity of developing the full power of his imagination.

In the summer he went to Carrara to superintend the quarrying of blocks of marble big enough for the tomb, and for eight months he remained inaccessible in that awe-inspiring landscape, surrounded by stone. These long sojourns in Carrara, repeated several times in his life, were to Michelangelo like religious activity. He returned to Rome in the winter of 1505-1506, ready to concentrate all his force on executing his grandiose ideas. Then there occurred the first catastrophe in what, since Condivi, all writers on Michelangelo have called the tragedy of the tomb. Pope Julius refused to see him. It was Michelangelo's first experience of court intrigue and of the readiness with which princes allow themselves to be swayed by rival coteries. Later in life he accepted such intrigues with a firm and melancholy stoicism. But to the young man of thirty-one, his mind charged with colossal images, his spirit burning like a fire, this treachery was intolerable; and in April, 1506, he left Rome without a word and returned to Florence. For seven months the Pope tried to lure him back to Rome, but Michelangelo was suspicious and the Florentine government protected him. Finally, when the Pope conquered Bologna in November, Michelangelo felt bound to go there and ask for forgiveness, and there follows the scene I have already described. I should add that although Condivi says that he had this account from Michelangelo's own lips, contemporary documents suggest that the artist was considerably more penitent. Almost as a penance, he was commissioned to make a gigantic bronze statue of the Pope to go over the door of San Petronio in Bologna. It cost him one of the most miserable and unproductive years of his life; and shortly after it had been put in place, was broken up and melted down for the bronze.

At the beginning of March, 1508, he left Bologna for Florence, intending to settle down in his native town and complete the commissions that he had left unfinished there. He thought that he was "free of Rome"; but within two months his terrible old master had forced him to return there. What was worse, Julius did not allow him to finish the tomb, but gave him a new and in many ways unsuitable commission, to paint the ceiling of the papal chapel in the Vatican, know as the Sistine. Michelangelo's early biographers believed that the proposal was put forward by his enemy, Bramante, in order to discredit him; and it is true that Michelangelo accepted the commission under protest, complaining that painting was not his art. Documents show, however, that the proposal had been discussed two years earlier; and there is no doubt that Michelangelo had practiced painting. The *Holy Family* in the Uffizi, known as the Doni *tondo,* dates from 1504; and as an apprentice to Ghirlandaio he seems to have had a hand in the frescoes of Santa Maria Novella.

It was not as a technical, but as an intellectual feat that the Sistine ceiling involved such a vast extension of his faculties. Hitherto his sculptures had been concerned with single figures or traditional themes, and in the *Battle of Cascina,* the subject had been only a pretext for a pictorial exercise. Now he had to illustrate the first phase of human destiny, and what theologians called the world *ante legem.* He was no longer concerned with problems of form alone, but with problems of philosophy.

In the chief history paintings of the Renaissance, the artist was usually given a "program" by his patron or some attendant poet or philosopher. But Michelangelo, in a well-known letter, explains that he was told to work out his subject for himself. Even he could not conceive the whole theme in a single flash of inspiration.

A QUARREL WITH THE POPE

A LETTER FROM MICHELANGELO TO THE PAPAL ARCHITECT GIULIANO DA SANGALLO, SENT FROM FLORENCE IN 1506.

I learn from a letter sent by you that the Pope was angry at my departure, that he is willing to place the money at my disposal and to carry out what was agreed upon between us; also, that I am to come back and fear nothing.

As far as my departure is concerned, the truth is that on Holy Saturday I heard the Pope, speaking at table with a jeweler and the Master of the Ceremonies, say that he did not want to spend another baiocco on stones whether small or large, which surprised me very much. However, before I set out, I asked him for some of the money required for the continuance of my work. His Holiness replied that I was to come back again on Monday, and I went on Monday, and on Tuesday, and on Wednesday, and on Thursday,—as His Holiness saw. At last, on the Friday morning, I was turned out, that is to say, I was driven away; and the person who turned me away said he knew who I was, but that such were his orders. Thereupon, having heard those words on Saturday and seeing them afterward put into execution, I lost all hope. But this alone was not the whole reason of my departure. There was also another cause but I do not wish to write about it; enough that it made me think that, if I were to remain in Rome, my own tomb would be prepared before that of the Pope. This is the reason for my sudden departure.

Now you write to me on behalf of the Pope, and in similar manner you will read this letter to the Pope. Give his Holiness to understand that I am more eager to proceed with the work than ever I was before, and that if he really wishes to have this tomb erected it would be well for him not to vex me as to where the work is to be done, provided that within the agreed period of five years it be erected in St. Peter's, on the site he shall choose, and it be a beautiful work, as I have promised: for I am persuaded that it be a work without an equal in all the world if it be carried out.

If His Holiness now wishes to proceed, let him deposit the said money here in Florence . . .

Both in subject and style it developed prodigiously as the work continued. Yet at some early point, Michelangelo recognized that the story of the Creation could be transformed from a fanciful narrative into a profound philosophy. He did so by compelling us to read his "histories" in a reverse order. Over our head, as we enter the chapel, is the *Drunkenness of Noah*; at the far end, over the altar, is the *Creation*. Thus the ceiling illustrates the Neoplatonic doctrine, so dear to Michelangelo, and so often expressed in his sonnets, that life must be a progression from the servitude of the body to the liberation of the soul. It begins with the inert figure of Noah, where the body has taken complete possession, and ends with the figure of the Almighty dividing light from darkness, in which the body has been completely transformed into a symbol of the spirit, and even the head, with its too evident human associations, has become indistinct.

The same evolution, both of spirit and style, can be seen in the so-called athletes, those deeply personal creations which come first to most people's minds at the mention of Michelangelo. They are not, as used to be supposed, mere decoration, but symbolize the thoughts of the prophets and seers in the spandrels and are a link between them and the histories. But because this subject is limited to the representation of a single naked youth, we are made more conscious of changes in style. At first they are classical in the narrow sense. They are symmetrical, bound by a firm outline, forming a closed rhythm, and several are actually derived from antique gems. The athletes on the middle of the ceiling, beside the *Creation of Eve,* are already less symmetrical and the unity of planes has been abandoned. In the last pair of athletes, those beside the *Creation of Light,* a balanced and reciprocal movement is entirely abandoned, and Michelangelo has created a continuous movement which twists round the central scene.

In the use of this twisting rhythm he is realizing an experience which he had stored away in his mind almost five years earlier, the impact of the famous antique group known as the *Laocoön*. It had been discovered in January, 1506, and Michelangelo had been one of the first to identify and admire it. No doubt he

recognized immediately that it confirmed his own feelings about
the potential expressiveness of the nude. But like most great poets
and artists, he had a long period of gestation, and it was not
till about 1510 that a reminiscence of the *Laocoön* is perceptible in his work. Then, finally, in the corner spandrels de-
picting the *Crucifixion of Hamar* and the *Brazen Serpent*, this
new system of form, in which tormented rhythms and violent
foreshortening are used to express mental and physical agony, is
pushed to a limit never surpassed. By 1511 Michelangelo had
anticipated almost every extremity of style which would engage the ingenuity of mannerist and baroque artists in the next
hundred years.

Two years before the ceiling was completed it had begun to
make itself felt by premonitory rumbling, like those which antici-
pate the theme in the last movement of Beethoven's Ninth Sym-
phony. Raphael himself had been smuggled in by Bramante, and
had immediately added a Michelangelesque figure to the already
complete design of his fresco of the *School of Athens*.

When, on October 31, 1512, the frescoes were officially unveiled, artists and connoisseurs were prepared for something which
should change the course of painting; and that, in fact, is what it
did; and not only painting, but the whole mode of feeling. The
freshness and wonder of the early Renaissance, the delight in
living things unburdened with a conscience, birds, children, flowers—all this was crushed by the oppressive awareness of human
destiny. And instead of a natural ease of arrangement in which
flower was set beside flower and face beside face, there came
into being the new unity of struggle, the unity of Hercules grap-
pling with the lion.

On October 31, 1512, when the ceiling was finally unveiled,
Michelangelo was thirty-seven. He lived to be eighty-nine. In this
half century he executed some of his greatest works—the marble
prisoners, the Medici tombs, the *Last Judgment,* the marvelous
and tragic Pietàs of his old age. The mood becomes graver; the
confidence in physical beauty diminishes, and is at last rejected
with a kind of horror. But fundamentally there is an unvarying

aim; to use the human body as an instrument with which to reveal the ascent of the human soul. The body must perish: and Michelangelo became increasingly preoccupied with death; the soul must be judged; and he became more and more burdened by the consciousness of sin. But in his imagination body and soul remain indivisible, fatally united in their struggle; and out of this involvement he creates movements, gestures, limbs, proportions which allow us poor worldlings, with our sordid material interests, to become, through the contemplation of form, momentarily capable of spiritual life.

IV.

Lorenzo de' Medici

by RALPH ROEDER

Lorenzo de' Medici was, first and last, a financier; he was much more besides—politician, statesman, patron of art and letters—but these were merely functions of the financier developed by his forefathers, which he inherited together with the fortune of his family, and in each of these roles his performance was the consummation of theirs. His biography begins before he was born, and he sits for his portrait under his family tree.

His great-grandfather, Giovanni di Bicci de' Medici, was the first millionaire of the family. Of plebeian origin, the Medici had risen by prosperous trade to the front rank of the *nobili popolani*—the merchant princes of the major guilds—but they had not abandoned the class from which they sprang, and it served them steadily in their subsequent ascent to power. The banking business which Giovanni built up with branches in sixteen European capitals entitled him to a leading position among the eighty banking firms of Florence, and would have assuerd him a corresponding influence in the government had he chosen to claim it, since the bankers' guild supplied the capital and the connections for the enterprises of the state; but Giovanni was prudent and avoided politics. Retiring by nature, modest and unassuming, he spent his money on the construction of churches, the encouragement of art, and works of charity (the Foundling Hospital built for him by Brunelleschi, and the church of San Lorenzo rebuilt for him by the great architect as a family temple, were his monuments), and as long as he confined his public spirit to such modest activities, he passed for a safe man and honors came to him unsought. Summoned to the Signory, he revealed a different form of public spirit, however, by supporting against powerful opposition a tax reform, which substituted for the universal poll tax and the arbitrary assessments of the past a 1½ per cent levy on capital. This innovation was a boon for the poor, who reckoned it among his major charities; and since it was enacted when an unsuccessful war was about to be resumed and the tax rate raised, it won him high favor with the little people; but it incensed the rich. "Since the burden was to be distributed by law and not by men," Machiavelli, the official biographer of the family, observed, "it weighed heavily on the powerful citizens and was received with extreme displeasure by the mighty." Their anger rose and turned to alarm when the little people proposed to make the reform retroactive to compensate the losses they had suffered in the past; but Giovanni dissuaded them from this abuse of his bounty, and having done his duty impartially by both sides, retired to private life and the practice of his private charities. When he retired to the grave in 1429, he was widely missed and mourned by those whom he benefited.

The eldest son of this model Medici followed closely in his footsteps. Equally modest and unassuming and no less charitable, Cosimo also minded his own business carefully; but that business was constantly growing, and with it the motives to ruin it. The rich had not forgotten the tax reform imposed on them by his benevolent father, nor the fund of good will he won with his churches and his charities. For four years Cosimo was not molested, but in 1433 the blow fell. The Albizzi, a rival family which had long been conspiring with the former nobles to uproot the upstart Medici, judged the moment ripe to strike. Before a Signory predisposed in their favor and a *gonfaloniere* in their debt, they preferred charges against the opulent family as a danger to the state because of their wealth and ambition. Among other proof, they cited a new mansion which Cosimo was building on a scale and in a style unbefitting a private citizen. The evidence, based on prejudice and suspicion, prospered; Cosimo was arrested and imprisoned. The Albizzi, bent on obtaining the death penalty, summoned a popular assembly to appoint by acclamation a *balia* —a commission created in emergencies and entrusted with absolute power for a limited length of time—and the *balia,* composed of two hundred leading citizens, deliberated without reaching a decision. Many were for death, many for banishment, many more, moved by compassion or fear, were silent. For four days the prisoner refused food until a friendly jailer shared it with him; with his jailer's help he smuggled a substantial bribe to the *gonfaloniere,* and the sentence was commuted to banishment for himself and his family for ten years. A year later, a friendly Signory canceled the decree and recalled him. "Seldom," said Machiavelli, "has a citizen returning from a great victory been greeted by such a concourse of people and with such demonstrations of affection as Cosimo on his return from exile." The Albizzi, after failing to seize the government by force before his return, fled, two hundred of their partisans were banished or fled, and when Cosimo was reproached for so drastic a purge of prominent citizens, he replied that new nobles could be made with two lengths of crimson cloth and that states were not ruled by Paternosters. "Better a city destroyed than lost," he added.

As a result of this experience, and to prevent its recurrence, Cosimo sought and secured a controlling influence in the government. The forms of the republic were respected and adapted to his purpose. Profiting by the reaction in his favor, he served a brief term as *gonfaloniere,* but soon abandoned public office in favor of a less conspicuous but far more permanent and powerful position as banker to the republic and confidential adviser to the government. His foes having fled, his friends assumed office, and he kept them there by the customary methods of the politician. One was purely Florentine—the *balia*—employed whenever a direct appeal to the people was needed to support his authority, but discarded when he was so firmly established that he could afford to restore normal elections and humor his enemies by the free play of Florentine democracy. The other was money, universally valid in all times and places. Reviving the famous tax reform of his father, which had fallen into disuse, and enforcing it in favor of his friends and against his foes, he wielded it as a defensive and offensive weapon more deadly than daggers.

Neither of these methods would have availed him long, however—and they served him for thirty years—had he not identified his interests completely with those of the state and guided and guarded them wisely and well. As banker to the commonwealth, he put the republic in his pocket by liberal loans and assumed many public expenses himself to lend it luster and prestige. He entertained distinguished visitors at his own expense and went out of his way to attract them to Florence when they were worth it. On one such occasion he traveled to Ferrara where a council of the Pope, the Primate of the Eastern Church, and one of the last Byzantine emperors was sitting, and induced them to transfer their deliberations to Florence, where he lodged them magnificently and converted the city for a season into a brilliant political, religious, cultural, and commercial convention town. The council accomplished nothing, but it left a lasting impression on Florence, where the painter Benozzo Gozzoli commemorated the sumptuous exotic costumes of the Eastern dignitaries on the walls of the Medici chapel.

In foreign affairs Cosimo took the same risks as a statesman. Like his father, he loved peace and avoided war, and with a single exception he made war to secure peace. Reversing the traditional alliance with Venice against their mutual enemy, the aggressive duchy of Milan, he supplied a soldier of fortune, Francesco Sforza, with money and means to overthrow the Visconti dynasty, and won an equally peace-loving friend in their place; and when Venice and Naples turned against him, he paralyzed their military operations by calling in his loans.

Again like his father, he was a great builder of churches and a liberal patron of art. Architects of the stature of Brunelleschi and Michelozzo, sculptors of the grace of Donatello and Luca della Robbia, painters of the demure splendor of Fra Angelico, Filippo Lippi, and Benozzo Gozzoli, worked for him building or adorning his monuments—the monastery of San Marco, the church of San Lorenzo, the Medici palace, among others—and he added to his laurels by the encouragement of learning. Learning he encouraged with the curiosity of close acquaintance, for he was uncommonly well educated. He maintained agents abroad searching for rare prizes to fill his library and found the best at home: the Bishop of Bologna, a fellow collector who borrowed from his purse to satisfy his passion for books, repaid his debt first by cataloguing his library and later, when he became Pope Nicholas V, by awarding the management of the papal finances to the Medici bank in Rome, whose books showed a fair profit in the Jubilee year of 1450.

But it was in the art of politics that Cosimo shone. Studiously effacing himself and remaining in the background of government, he was recognized, nevertheless, both at home and abroad as the real Head of State—*Capa della Repubblica*—by virtue of financial sovereignty and adroit brainwork with the support of armed force. Living simply and soberly, he reached the ripe old age of seventy-five, but as he aged he was crippled by gout, his grip on the government weakened, and his last days were darkened by fear for the future of his family. Of his two sons, one was a chronic invalid and the other died before he did; and he was heard to murmur as he was borne through the rooms of that mansion which almost cost him his life, "Too large a house for so small a family." His fears were well founded, for his grandsons were mere boys; and his party, loyal and obedient while it was curbed by opposition, became unruly and insolent as soon as resistance subsided, and outraged Florence by unbridled oppression, corruption, and excesses which, weary, old, and infirm, he could no longer control and which threatened to wreck his lifework. It was a tribute to his own moderation and political tact that he preserved public respect to the end, and when he was laid to rest with his father in 1464, his countrymen inscribed on the tomb of the man who had given them thirty years of domestic peace and external stability the title PATER PATRIAE.

The second model Medici left a son, Piero, hampered by gout, the indolence of an invalid, a mild disposition, and perfidious advisers. Finding that his father's liberality had left his financial affairs in confusion and disorder, he consulted a trusted friend of his father's, who advised him to call in his loans, counting on a panic to wrest the state from his hands. Piero fell into the trap, many business failures followed, and he was denounced by his debtors as an ungrateful miser and accused of jeopardizing the properity of Florence to protect his capital; but he survived this blow as well as two attempts to overthrow him by force of arms.

His five brief years as head of state, marred by civil dissension, saw one event which was to set the reputation of his son and successor. So well had Cosimo gilded the Florentine lily that Louis XI of France conferred on Piero the right to add the French fleur-de-lis to the five red balls of the Medici coat of arms, and Piero took advantage of the favor. He married his nineteen-year-old son Lorenzo into the house of Orsini, one of the great feudal families of Rome, but as this was a departure from custom (Cosimo had made it a rule to marry the Medici at home), the match was unpopular in Florence. Malcontents complained that the ambition of the rising bourgeois was unbounded, that the city was no longer big enough for the citizen, that the Medici were satisfied with nothing less than a foreign and baronial alliance, and that they would soon be assuming the style of princes themselves. The betrothal was celebrated by a tournament, an aristocratic spectacle so foreign and unfamiliar in Florence that Machiavelli felt it necessary to explain it: ". . . a scuffle of men on horseback in which the leading young men of the city contended with the most renowned cavaliers of Italy; and among the Florentine youth the most famous was Lorenzo, who carried off the prize not by favor but by his own valor." Gorgeously accoutered in ornate armor, bearing the French fleur-de-lis on his shield and the Medici device on his banner, the powerful young athlete unhorsed all his opponents easily, and the pride which his countrymen took in his prowess reconciled them to his marriage. It was celebrated splendidly, and his father, who had once been called a miser, made ample amends with the wedding feast. As Machiavelli added slyly, "Piero decided to celebrate the nuptials of his son Lorenzo with Clarice of the house of Orsini magnificently, and they were held with the pomp of apparel and all other manner of magnificence befitting such a man." Long before he earned the title of Magnificent, Lorenzo learned its political value and developed an appetite for it.

Such was the heritage of Lorenzo de' Medici. "Two days after the death of my father," he wrote in later life, "although I, Lorenzo, was very young, being only in my twenty-first year, the principal men of the city and the state came to our house to condole on our loss and encourage me to take on myself the care of the city and the state, as my father and grandfather had done. This proposal being contrary to the instincts of my youthful age and considering that the burden and danger were great, I consented unwillingly, but I did so to protect our friends and our property, for it fares ill in Florence with anyone who possesses great wealth without any control in the government." *I, Lorenzo!* How lonely, how isolated the identification! More fortunate than his father, however, he found faithful friends who rallied to him loyally, and it was due to their devotion that he succeeded him peacefully. With the backing of a body of eminent citizens bent on banishing civil dissension from Florence, he began governing under singularly favorably conditions, and the first years were fairly easy—peaceful at home and only briefly disturbed abroad.

For nine years Lorenzo was indeed the most fortunate of his family. His father had been called the most mediocre of the Medici, because of his mild disposition; but no one could cast that slur on his son. Sheltered by his family tree and with no opposition to overcome, Lorenzo encountered only critics. Guicciardini was one of them, and he echoed many others. Lorenzo, he said, "desired glory and excellence above all other men and can be criticized for having had too much ambition even in minor things; he did not want to be equaled or imitated even in verses or games or exercises and turned angrily on anyone who did so." Unlike his father and grandfather, who were mature men when they became heads of the house, he was in the first flush of youth, and youth claimed its privileges of pleasure and the carefree enjoyment of life. Besides his other accomplishments, he was a poet —another variation from his breed, for though his ancestors took many risks they never ventured to write verses—and he composed fluently for festive occasions. Improving on his father, he entertained Florence continually with masquerades and revels, pageants and processions, engaging the best artists to design the masks and decorate the floats,and taking part in them himself; for these he wrote his *Trionfi,* his *Canzoni a Ballo,* and best of all, his famous carnival songs. Later historians were scandalized by the obscenity of these songs and lamented that Lorenzo catered to the taste of the common people, forgetting that Lorenzo was young, virile, and lusty. The tournament was an aristocratic entertainment; these spectacles preserved his ties with the people. A more serious charge was raised by his elders, who professed to see in these lighthearted frolics a profound political design to beguile the people and divert them from public affairs, as his father had done; but this was to credit him with sagacity beyond his years and needless guile, for these were untroubled times of peace and plenty, and public affairs went well. If ever history could be happy, it was then, and wisely he made the most of life while he could sing:

> *How passing fair is youth,*
> *Forever fleeting away;*
> *Who happy would be, let him be;*
> *Of tomorrow who can say?*

It was as if an uneasy premonition of doom prompted the haunting refrain; for, in fact, the triumph of time was approaching.

In every generation plots had been laid to ruin his family;

they were part of his heritage; and his turn came, long belated, in 1478, with the most formidable threat of all—the Pazzi conspiracy. The Pazzi were an old and numerous family with aristocratic pretensions superior to those of the Medici, and they had old scores to settle with Lorenzo.

Wealthy and proud, the Pazzi had been denied public office and the honors to which they were entitled, and they bore discrimination and abuse bitterly. The most sensitive of the family, Francesco, unable to suffer any longer, fled to Rome, where he fell in with a nephew of one of the most grasping and turbulent of the popes, and between them they hatched a plot for their mutual benefit. As ambitious as he was lowborn, Pope Sixtus IV was burdened with six covetous nephews, three of whom he placed profitably in the Church and a fourth in Imola, one of the poorest and smallest of the papal fiefs. When Francesco proposed to create a vacancy in Florence, Sixtus fell in with the scheme and consented to second the Pazzi in ousting the Medici. Thus encouraged, Francesco returned to Florence to enlist his family. Jacopo de' Pazzi, the head of the house, hesitated until he was convinced that the scheme had the blessing and the backing of the Pope.

The scheme was senseless on the face of it. A foreign potentate aiming to add Florence to the papal domain and impose a papal cub on a fiercely freedom-loving people, and relying on a Florentine family ambitious to fill the vacancy themselves—the plot was a patchwork of cross-purposes perfectly calculated to fail. Yet it nearly succeeded.

The Pope opened hostilities by canceling the concession of the Medici bank in Rome and transfering it to the Pazzi; then he lent a helping hand to the plot by appointing as Archbishop of Pisa a member of another family hostile to the Medici, the Salviati. Notwithstanding these unfriendly acts, Lorenzo seems to have suspected nothing, although he refused Salviati admission to his see. In April, 1478, the conspirators assembled in Florence and were hospitably entertained in Lorenzo's villa at Fiesole, where they planned to kill him during a banquet. However, his brother

Giuliano was absent, and since the murder of both was essential to success, they postponed the blow until the following morning, during the celebration of High Mass in the Duomo, where both were bound to appear for the celebration of Easter Sunday. The change created an unforeseen difficulty; the hired assassin suffered an attack of conscientious scruples and shrank from committing sacrilege as well as murder in the cathedral; Francesco de' Pazzi, a priest, and an accomplice assumed his duties, but still another hitch developed. Giuliano was missing when the service began, and they were forced to fetch him to the slaughter, coaxing him out of bed, where he was nursing a bad knee. They braced him between them, embracing him fondly and feeling his body to make sure that he was unarmed, and brought the laggard limping to the altar; then, having finally united the victims, they struck. The church was crowded; the signal for attack was the solemn moment when the Cardinal who was officiating (another papal cub but not privy to the plot) raised the Host and hundreds of heads bowed devoutly. Giuliano bent obediently, the priest behind his back struck the first blow, and Francesco finished him off with eighteen more—so furiously that he hacked himself in the leg and in the confusion was mistaken for one of the victims. Lorenzo defended himself, escaped with a gash in the neck, and ran into the sacristy, where his friends bolted the doors and waited for help. In the meanwhile Archbishop Salviati, entrusted with the most difficult part of the undertaking, entered the palace to seize the government. His confederates waited below in the chancery, where they locked themselves in by mistake, while he mounted to the upper floor to parley with the Signory, but his agitation betrayed him and aroused their suspicion, and before he could summon assistance the *gonfaloniere* hanged him, stammering, from the window. The city was now in an uproar. Francesco de' Pazzi, weak from loss of blood, took to his bed and begged his uncle to rally the people to their cause. Sallying forth with a hundred armed men, Jacopo de' Pazzi roamed the streets raising the cry of *Liberty!* without arousing a response, and running into a mob acclaiming the Balls, abandoned the attempt and fled. Lorenzo, escorted by his friends, returned home unharmed.

The mob avenged him loyally. Francesco de' Pazzi, dragged from his bed, was hanged beside the body of the Archbishop, dangling limply with a cluster of comrades overhead. A furious manhunt followed: everyone remotely connected with the conspiracy or suspected of sympathizing with it was brought to justice or mobbed; seventy perished in the first four days and two hundred more before the tumult subsided. Jacopo de' Pazzi, caught and killed, was not allowed to rest in his grave: a horde of scavenging boys unearthed his body, dragged it through the streets, and flung it naked into the Arno. Of his ten sons and nephews, two were beheaded; one was saved by Lorenzo, who was his brother-in-law; the survivors were sentenced to imprisonment or exile, and even the name Pazzi was wiped out by proscription.

Infuriated by the failure of the plot, the Pope demanded that Lorenzo surrender and that the Florentine government answer before an ecclesiastical court for the crime of sacrilege committed on the person of the Archbishop. Lorenzo protested that his only crime was that he had not allowed himself to be murdered; the Signory seconded him, circulated the confession of one of the conspirators exposing the complicity of the Pope, and appealed to the sovereigns of Europe for support. The sovereigns of Europe sided with the Medici; the Pope excommunicated the Florentine state; the Florentine clergy outlawed him in turn; the Pope declared war. Brandishing both his spiritual and temporal arms, he forbade the faithful to trade with the rebellious republic, broke their previous alliances, prohibited any state from forming new ones or any soldier from taking service with them, and summoned to his assistance the Sienese republic and his feudal ally the King of Naples; and their troops invaded Tuscany. The fortunes of war ran against the Florentines, and Lorenzo, unwilling to tax the loyalty of his people, volunteered to surrender himself, but the issue had long since outgrown a personal sacrifice and the Signory refused to abandon him. He insisted, however, slipped off to Pisa, and sailed for Naples to treat with King Ferrante. Ferrante was a notoriously treacherous monarch, but, impressed by Lorenzo's daring, he detained him less as a prisoner than as a guest, listened to his arguments, and consented to abandon the

Pope. The Pope fumed, but an incursion of the Turks in Calabria compelled him, like Ferrante, to make peace.

The Pazzi conspiracy, formidable in its folly, failed; but it created a crisis and marked a turning point in Lorenzo's political career. To prevent its recurrence, he surrounded himself with an armed guard and adopted those precautions which his enemies denounced as a tyranny. He tightened his grip on the government, subordinated the Signory and the councils to a self-perpetuating privy council responsible to himself alone, and converted the controlling influence created by Cosimo into absolute personal rule. Before the Pazzi conspiracy, he was the most fortunate of the Medici; after it, the most masterful; and *I, Lorenzo* now assumed its full meaning for Florence. But the crisis had a further effect; it stimulated his powers as a statesman, and he devoted them diligently to preserving the balance of power and keeping the peace in Italy.

No sooner was the crisis over than his critics found fault with his conduct. The expedition to Naples was blamed as a rash, foolhardy, and unnecessary adventure. It was argued that he could have attained the same success sitting safely at home, instead of risking his life in the hands of a faithless enemy and returning to Florence as a hero. Also, instead of antagonizing the Pope and playing the injured party, if he had concealed his grievance and handled him gently he might have averted a war that caused the greatest damage to the city, especially in trade and taxes. Also his punishment of the Pazzi was excessively cruel. By some he was considered unnaturally vindictive and heartless for imprisoning the innocent young men of the family and preventing the Pazzi girls from marrying and breeding more of their kind; although Guicciardini admitted that "the event was so bitter that it is no wonder that he was extraordinarily angered by it. And it was seen later that, softened by time, he gave permission for the maidens to marry and was willing to release the Pazzi from prison and let them go and live outside of Florentine territory. And also it was seen that he did not employ cruelty in other matters and was not a blood-thirsty person." But while suspicion lingered, and it lingered long, he intervened vigilantly in domestic affairs, preventing powerful families from intermarrying, arranging matches to suit himself, and permitting no important marriage in Florence without his intervention and consent.

No sooner was peace restored than he returned to his pleasures and won his final and most undeniable triumphs in their pursuit— the pursuit of art and letters and the pursuit of women. In both he was resolved to excel. The lover of art and letters more than maintained the fame of his family—he increased it by his boundless liberality. Under his enlightened lead Florence became the mother of arts and the cultural capital of Italy, imitated but unsurpassed by rival states. He set the pace, and other princes were compelled to compete; but he was the highest bidder for the services of scholars and artists and carried off all the prizes for the glory of Florence and the greater glory of the Medici. In Pisa he founded a superfluous branch of the University of Florence for the sheer pleasure of surpassing rival schools, paying highest salaries and sparing neither trouble nor expense to secure the most famous teachers in Italy. In Florence the Platonic Academy formed part of his household and boasted the best philosophers he could find. Sharing the craze for ancient learning which was widening the mental horizon of his age, he introduced it even into his home and made philosophy a household word, collecting intellectuals at his table to discuss it and teach Florence that no one could live without it. He could not. "When my mind is disturbed by the tumult of public affairs and my ears are stunned by the clamor of turbulent citizens," he confessed to a friend, "how could I bear such dissensions unless I found relief in learning?" Study was a refuge from politics and an escape from statecraft. Educated as a boy by humanists, he was one of them and collected them to preserve the most precious of his treasures, his peace of mind. His Poggio, his Poliziano, his Pico della Mirandola, his Marsilio Ficino, were bosom friends who formed his intellectual family. On books alone he spent more than half the annual income of the state, and for art his bounty was unbounded. Ambitious to be the most universal as well as the most glorious of the

Medici, he befriended all the arts, and they flourished abundantly at his bidding. "For vernacular poetry, music, architecture, painting, sculpture, and all the fine and mechanical arts he showed the same favor, so that the city overflowed with all these graces," Guicciardini acknowledged. Artists flocked to Florence from far and near, attracted by the magnetic name of Lorenzo de' Medici. Not merely for pecuniary reward, either, for he was a connoisseur who appreciated their gifts, understood their problems, and defended them against fools. When someone found fault with the music of Squarcialupi, he scolded the critic as sensitively as if he were the composer himself.) "If only you knew how difficult it is to attain perfection in any art!" he admonished.

When it came to his other ruling passion, Guicciardini found it difficult to forgive his fidelity to it: "He was licentious and very amorous and constant in his loves, which usually lasted several years. In the opinion of many, this so weakened his body that it caused him to die comparatively young. His last love, which endured many years, was for Bartolommea de' Nasi, wife of Donato Benci, who was by no means beautiful but with a style and grace of her own. . . . What folly that a man of such great reputation and prudence, forty years old, should be so infatuated with a woman who was not beautiful and already well along in years, that he was led to do what would be disgraceful in any boy!" Physically, also, he found fault with him: "Lorenzo was of medium height, his countenance coarse and dark in color, yet with an air of dignity; his voice and pronunciation harsh and unpleasing, because he spoke through his nose." But the fact remains that he was attractive to women; neither his nasal voice nor his coarse features nor his swarthy complexion nor the natural blemishes with which he was born were displeasing to them.

As he matured he mellowed and became as tolerant of his critics as they expected him to be. Though Guicciardini was one of them, he was the most indulgent and judicious of his judges, and his final verdict was fair. "Though the city was not free under him, it would have been impossible to find a better or more pleasing tyrant. From his natural goodness and inclination came

infinite advantages, but through the necessity of tyranny some evils
although they were restrained and limited as much as necessity
permitted . . ."

Twelve uneventful years followed the Pazzi conspiracy, cloudless
and carefree until Lorenzo succumbed to gout and to another,
graver affliction. He neglected his financial affairs, which fell
into confusion and disorder, and the fall was fatal. Machiavelli
blamed his misfortunes on mismanagement by his banking agents
abroad, stating that Lorenzo, to avoid further reverses, abandoned
his mercantile enterprises and turned instead to "possessions, as
a more stable and firm form of wealth." Among his possessions
was the state, and his forays into the public coffers played havoc
with the public finances. Insolvency became so acute that in 1490
a commission was created to reform the fiscal administration of
Florence; the currency, hitherto the most stable in Europe, was
depreciated to a fifth of its face value; and the government was
driven to desperate measures to avoid bankruptcy. Lorenzo was
just enough of a financier to save his private fortune by with-
drawing it from commerce and investing in real estate, but at
the cost of his good name. Financial acumen was the foundation
of the Medici political fortunes, and he who lacked it was exposed
to the ruin which the enemies of his house had tried to vain to
bring about for three generations.

Under these gathering clouds, his last days were also darkened
by a new adversary. An alien agitator raised his voice in Florence
to echo the complaints of his enemies and disturb his peace of
mind; the sermons of Savonarola kindled contention anew and in
an unexpected quarter. From the pulpit of San Marco—a Medici
foundation—a foreign reformer called Lorenzo to account for
his political sins. The festivities with which Lorenzo entertained
Florence were denounced as political snares: "The tyrant is wont
to busy his people with spectacles and festivities, that they may
think of their pastimes and not of his designs, and becoming
unaccustomed to the conduct of the commonwealth, leave the
reins of government in his hands." The charge, old and familiar
though it was, could no longer be ignored in the gloom of chang-

ing times, and it was followed by graver ones. Summoned to preach before the Signory, Savonarola said: "Tyrants are incorrigible because they are proud, because they love flattery, because they will not restore their ill-gotten gains. They allow bad officials to have their way; they yield to adulation; they neither heed the poor nor condemn the rich; they expect peasants and paupers to work for them gratis or they tolerate officials who do so; they farm out the taxes to aggravate the people more and more . . . The people are oppressed by taxes, and when they come to pay unbearable sums, the rich cry; Give me the rest . . . When widows come weeping, they are told: Go to sleep. When the poor complain, they are told: Pay, pay." The preacher was popular, his following grew, and in the Lent of 1491 he moved into the Duomo, where, before a congregation packed to the doors, he preached inflammatory sermons which terrified his hearers, predicting a coming calamity, ordained by divine wrath, which would sweep away the princes of Italy, including the Medici and all their iniquities. Lorenzo was tolerant, but he was troubled: what the Pazzi failed to accomplish, the prophet promised to perform. He made advances to mollify him, but he was rebuffed. He sent a delegation to reason with him. They hinted at banishment. "Tell Lorenzo to do penance for his sins," Savonarola replied, "for God will punish him and his. I do not fear your banishments. Though I am a stranger here and he a citizen, and the foremost in the city, I shall remain and he will go. I shall remain," he repeated proudly, "and he will go." And he foretold the death of Lorenzo within a year.

A year later Lorenzo lay dying in his villa at Careggi. He was in great pain, suffering from an abdominal disorder aggravated by his physicians, who fed him powdered pearls, and he sent for Savonarola to relieve his soul. Savonarola came. According to a popular but probably apocryphal account of the scene, the priest's price of salvation included the restoration of all ill-gotten gains and the restitution of liberty to Florence; to the first Lorenzo agreed, but he gave up the ghost and expired unabsolved before he could consent to the second.

Machiavelli was kinder. He acquitted Lorenzo of his political sins for the sake of the statesman whom Florence had lost, and acquitted him in a bountiful obituary. "Of Fortune and of God he was supremely loved, wherefore all his enterprises ended well and those of his enemies ill . . . All the citizens mourned his death and all the princes of Italy . . . and that they had good reason to grieve the result soon showed; for Italy being deprived of his counsels, none of those who remained found any means of curbing or satisfying the ambition of Lodovico Sforza, the governor of the Duke of Milan . . . as soon as Lorenzo died, all those bad seeds began to sprout which not long after, he who could quell them being no longer alive, ruined and are still ruining Italy."

And so it proved. Lorenzo was the pivot of Italian politics, and his eldest son, Piero, was born to be unfortunate—for himself, for his family, and for Florence. Two years after the death of Lorenzo, a revolt broke out, the Medici were driven into exile, and their palace sacked by a mob of vandals. Of Lorenzo nothing was left but the memory. The financier was a failure, the politician and the statesman were ephemeral, and of all the titles to fame which he left on deposit for posterity, only the patron of culture was remembered as Lorenzo the Magnificent.

V.

Leonardo da Vinci

by J. BRONOWSKI

Leonardo was born outside the small town of Vinci, near Florence, in 1452; the traditional date of his birthday is April 15. The birthday is hardly worth remembering, but the year is, for its remoteness remains a constant surprise. Leonardo's gifts speak so directly, his imagination is so immediate to us, that we have to remind ourselves with an effort that he was born more than five hundred years ago. He lived long before William Shakespeare and Rembrandt and Isaac Newton. Leonardo was dead before Nicolaus Copernicus felt sure that the earth goes around the sun; he was an old man, unhappy and full of regrets, when Martin Luther began the Reformation; and he had already passed the turning point of middle life when Christopher Columbus discovered America.

Leonardo was the illegitimate son of a lawyer and a woman who may have been a servant in the house of Leonardo's grandparents. The boy's father did take several wives—each a member of a good Florentine family—but not for over twenty years were there any more children. Leonardo was thus his father's only child during those formative years.

Italians in the Renaissance were not outraged by the thought that a bright child had been conceived out of wedlock. Illegitimacy was a commonplace of the time; men were proud of making their own way; and churchmen and condottieri, artists and statesmen, boasted that they were born out of wedlock. This was no stigma among the thrusting, self-made men of the Renaissance; indeed, as the historian Jakob Burckhardt wrote, "The fitness of the individual, his worth and capacity, were of more weight than all the laws and usages which prevailed elsewhere in the West."

Nevertheless, we get the feeling that Leonardo never walked easily in the houses of the great, and that this wariness goes back to his childhood. There is something hooded and withdrawn about his character which calls up a picture of a child made much of and yet not at home in the house of his birth. All his life he hated to see suffering. The story is told of Leonardo buying birds in the market place, holding them in his hand for a moment, and then setting them free. It is evident that in that rough, insensitive time he was one of the few men who could not bear to give pain to animals.

When Leonardo was about fourteen, his father apprenticed him to Andrea del Verrocchio, one of the foremost artists in Florence. The time was 1466 or thereabouts; Florence was aflower with wealth and splendor; its tone was set, its taste was led, by the great family of the Medici. Here the display of riches was more than a reward for success—it was almost a ritual, a public announcement of status and authority.

The *botteghe,* or workshops, of Verrocchio and other artists supplied this society with its beautiful treasures and trinkets. Verrocchio was a painter and sculptor, and was also a goldsmith and a decorator. His studio was, in an exact sense, a workshop, and it was Verrocchio's business to supply from it a picture or a chair, a statue or a goblet, a golden chafing dish or a ceremonial suit of armor. Verrocchio himself could turn his hand to all these things; however, he was a rather wooden painter, and he seems therefore to have turned more and more to sculpture.

One reason why Verrocchio could turn from painting was that his apprentice Leonardo was so good at it. The artist who ran his studio as a workshop had to conserve and to divide its labor intelligently and expediently; and when he had an apprentice who could paint, he gave him his head—and did something else himself. Tradition has it that Leonardo was still a boy when he painted an angel in one of Verrocchio's religious commissions, and made it more lifelike than his master could.

The story of the boy painter who outdoes his master is characteristic of the Renaissance; it is also told of Raphael and others. For this was an age in love with surprises, eager to discover genius, native and untaught. Yet the evidence is that the story is true of Leonardo. There is at least one picture by Verrocchio, *The Baptism of Christ,* in which one of the angels is unlike the rest, and has clearly been painted by a more sensitive and subtler hand. Moreover, the landscape of the *Baptism,* the detail of trees and grasses, has a vivid intimacy and an absorbed lucidness of vision which belong to no painter before Leonardo. There is at least one other painting by Verrocchio whose landscape shows the hand of Leonardo in the same way. Verrocchio must have known that the young Leonardo was not merely a better painter: he was a new painter.

Leonardo finished his training with Verrocchio about 1472, when he was twenty or so, and then went on working in Florence for another nine or ten years. He was good at other things besides painting. He is described as tall and handsome, graceful in all his actions, and apparently he had a fine singing voice, and the official records show that he was accused once of some homosexual scrape. (The evidence is that he lacked the usual sensual feelings for women, and tended rather to admire strong men.) He was interested in mathematics and mechanics, and particularly in the mechanics by which living things move: he constantly drew birds in flight, and he also made his first studies of human anatomy then.

These are odd interests in a painter, in the traditional sense; and yet they are inseparable from that desire to enter into the very structure of natural things which to Leonardo was the essence of painting. Later in life he wrote very simply about this:

And you who say that it is better to look at an anatomical dem-
onstration than to see these drawings, you would be right, if it were
possible to observe all the details shown in these drawings in a
single figure, in which, with all your ability, you will not see nor
acquire a knowledge of more than some few vains, while, in order
to obtain an exact and complete knowledge of these, I have dis-
sected more than ten human bodies, destroying all the various
members, and removing even the very smallest particles of the
flesh which surrounded these veins without causing any effusion
of blood other than the imperceptible bleeding of the capillary
veins. And, as one single body did not suffice for so long a time,
it was necessary to proceed by stages with so many bodies as
would render my knowledge complete; and this I repeated twice
over in order to discover the differences.

This is an account of work in anatomy, but it carries no hint of
a medical interest. For Leonardo did not want to cure men: he
wanted to know how their bodies are made and work. He distrusted the doctors of his time, and indeed the whole of medical
and chemical science then, which saw nature as an interplay of
occult qualities. Leonardo looked at nature directly, not through
the mind but through the eye. And his was a wonderful eye,
sharp and abrupt as a camera, which could stop a bird in flight
and fix the muscled movement of its wing. He wanted no specula-
tion about the soul of the bird, which scholars were still repeating
from Pythagoras; he wanted to understand the harsh mechanics
of its flight:

A bird is an instrument working according to mathematical law,
which instrument it is within the capacity of man to reproduce
with all its movements, but not with a corresponding degree of
strength, though it is deficient only in the power of maintaining
equilibrium. We may therefore say that such an instrument con-
structed by man is lacking in nothing except the life of the bird,
and this life must needs be supplied from that of man.

These preoccupations with the structure of things, with the
muscle under the skin and the bone under the muscle, seem to
have grown on Leonardo from the time that he began to work for

himself. They made him uninterested in, and perhaps unhappy with, the opportunities which Florence in the 1470's held out to artists who could display the warm beauty of the surface of things.

At this time Verrocchio was working on a statue of the great condottiere of Venice, Colleoni, and he left Florence to finish the work in Venice. Perhaps Leonardo felt that Florence was no longer the center of art it had once been. Or perhaps he could not resist the urge to create a statue better than Verrocchio's, for although he was not a sculptor, he wrote a long letter in 1482 to Lodovico Sforza in Milan, offering, among many other things, to make a statue of his father, the condottiere Francesco. In that same letter he described in detail his talents as a military engineer and inventor (two abilities likely to appeal to a Sforza), and soon after, at the age of thirty, he left Florence, carrying with him a silver lute that he had made in the shape of a horse's head, to spend nearly twenty years at the turbulent court of Milan.

Leonardo was in many respects self-taught, a self-willed man who did things almost truculently at times. Some of his paintings have perished as a result of ordinary bad luck, but others because of his insistence on mixing pigments with curious ingredients or on drying them in new and different ways. He was an innovator, an experimenter, a man never satisfied with the accepted or acceptable, and his decision to leave Florence was taken because Florence was a city of tradition, living on its golden dreams of the past.

We can only guess at the reasons for Leonardo's move from Florence to Milan. Yet if his reasons, intellectual and emotional, had any psychological coherence, it is clear enough what was the common strand in them. When Leonardo chose between Florence and Milan, he was not merely choosing between different cities: in a profound sense he was choosing between different cultures— between two different aspects of the Renaissance.

The Renaissance had begun, as its name implies, as a rebirth of a culture which had already been born once. It was, in the first place, a recovery of ancient learning, and the early Renaissance was not a revolution, but a revival.

Florence was above all the home of this classical revival. The medieval Church had leaned heavily on Aristotle, and had elevated him almost to the status of an honorary saint; now the Medici, in opposition, praised the work and the outlook of Plato. The pride of Florence was the Medici library of ancient manuscripts and commentaries on them, and the Platonic Academy. Florence in the 1470's, when Leonardo worked there, was dominated by the taste of the greatest of the Medici, Lorenzo the Magnificent, which was wholly classical and luxurious.

By contrast, Leonardo was one of the first men in whom the Renaissance expressed itself in a new way, not as a recovery but as a discovery. By the standards of Lorenzo, Leonardo was an unscholarly, unlettered painter: he did not even know Latin (he learned it later in Milan) and he never aspired to Greek. This is a subject to which he returned often and with heat in his notebooks:

I am fully aware that the fact of my not being a man of letters may cause certain arrogant persons to think that they may with reason censure me, alleging that I am a man ignorant of book-learning. Foolish folk! Do they not know that I might retort by saying, as did Marius to the Roman patricians, "They who themselves go about adorned in the labor of others will not permit me my own." They will say that because of my lack of book-learning, I cannot properly express what I desire to treat of. Do they not know that my subjects require for their exposition experience rather than the words of others? And since experience has been the mistress of whoever has written well, I take her as my mistress, and to her in all points make my appeal.

In this and other passages Leonardo is making two points. First, he is expressing his contempt for the new aristocracy of Florence, the moneyed men who lean on the talents of others, and whose taste, however authoritative, shows no mind of its own: "Whoever in discussion adduces authority uses not his intellect but rather memory." And second, Leonardo is setting up a new standard for the creation of works of art: the standard of the original mind that goes directly to nature, without intermediaries:

*The painter will produce pictures of little merit if he takes the
works of others as his standard; but, if he will apply himself to
learn from the objects of nature he will produce good results. This
we see was the case with the painters who came after the time of
the Romans, for they continually imitated each other, and from
age to age their art steadily declined. . . . it is safer to go direct to
the works of nature than to those which have been imitated from
her originals with great deterioration and thereby to acquire a bad
method, for he who has access to the fountain does not go to the
water-pot.*

In these quotations we have the crux of principle which divided
Leonardo from his predecessors in the Renaissance. The medieval
Church had taught that the universe can be understood only
spiritually, as a God-given and abstract order; that the beauty of
man and of nature is a snare which tempts us away from that
stark understanding. The Renaissance denied those morose dogmas,
holding instead that fleshly and natural beauty is not sinful, that
it is, on the contrary, an expression of the divine order. Yet the
form which this humanistic belief took was different at different
times. The pioneers of the Renaissance found their ideal of man
and nature in the splendid texts of the classics and in the works of
art of antiquity. But the new men of the Renaissance, the self-
taught and self-willed men like Leonardo, were not content with
anything at second hand. They wanted to see, to understand, to
enter into nature for themselves. Leonardo above all wanted not
to recover, but to discover, his own humanity.

When Leonardo left Florence, he was, therefore, turning his
back on the classical Renaissance. It was natural that he should
look for such men in Milan. Here was a city larger than Florence,
less dependent on its rich men, less self-satisfied, and with a more
cosmopolitan outlook toward the rest of Europe—particularly
toward France and toward Germany. Printing had been invented
before Leonardo was born, but hitherto had spread little into Italy;
now in the 1480's it became important in Milan. Mathematics
and mechanics, too, were more highly regarded in Milan than they
were in the Platonic climate of Florence. Leonardo all his life was

deeply drawn toward mathematics, and in Milan he drew the pictures for a book, *The Divine Proportion,* which the mathematician Luca Pacioli wrote and later printed. The divine proportion is that geometrical ratio which we now call the golden section, and it may be that this modern name was in fact first used for it by Leonardo da Vinci.

Intellectually, Leonardo was drawn to Milan because he was seeking a more downright and popular expression of Renaissance humanism than Florence offered. Emotionally, also, we sense that there was something about the brutal power of the court of Milan which attracted him more than the classical air of Florence. Lodovico Sforza was hardly a gracious man; yet something in the sinister directness of such a man, his naked drive to power, his simple and single will, plainly fascinated Leonardo. Like other sensitive men of the mind, he seems to have found a satisfaction in watching other men impose themselves ruthlessly on a world in which he himself was so ill at ease. We catch a hint of the same regard for male power in Leonardo's feelings for his model Giacomo Salai, whom he picked up in the streets of Milan, and whose endless misdeeds he forgave year in and year out with a tender and tolerant contempt.

This is another side of the search for the simplest, most rudimentary forces in man and in nature which took Leonardo to Milan. It made him accept the whims of Lodovico in a way in which he would not have accepted those of Lorenzo. Whatever his other faults may have been, Lodovico was an admirable patron. The fact that his patronage lacked the literary overtones of the Medici made it more attractive to Leonardo, and the variety of the work which Leonardo was called upon to perform at once appealed to his ingenuity, his curiosity, and his interest in experiment. In Milan, Leonardo became a busybody bending his great powers of invention to the trivial mechanics of court entertainment. He painted portraits of Lodovico's mistresses. He designed the costumes and devised the trick surprises of scenery for the court masques. To celebrate a visit of the King of France, he made an automaton shaped like a lion, which spilled a shower of lilies from its breast. He drew maps and proposed schemes of irrigation, he founded cannon and installed central heating, he planned engines of war and palaces, he designed a dozen schemes that Lodovico disregarded. And he went on making countless sketches of the most stupendous surprise of all, the statue of a rearing horse on which should sit Francesco Sforza, the soldier who had created the Milan that Lodovico now ruled. (It is interesting that he considered the animal the center of the monument, and that he should have referred to the statue simply as "the horse.") But like everything that Leonardo did for his patron, this also came to nothing.

Yet the years that Leonardo spent in Milan were not wasted. In an odd way, he could follow his bent here. The pageants and the plans that were expected of him can hardly have filled his time, and Lodovico was too busy with his ambitions to pester the court sculptor who had not finished his commission. In Milan, Leonardo did not have to work hard to earn his keep by doing the things that he knew how to do—above all, by painting. In one way this is a pity for us: we would have more great paintings, and fewer sketches, if Leonardo had had to deliver his work for cash during years in Milan, when his gifts flowed most easily. But in another way we can be grateful that Leonardo in those years of his middle life did not have to do the things he could do so well, which somehow were becoming distasteful to him. Leonardo in Milan grew impatient with his own gifts; he did not care to paint, he disliked the likeness that he could catch so swiftly, the tricks of light and shade, the surface appearances. His interest was more and more in the structure of things, and as a result his notebooks are now full of sketches which are always, as it were, taking nature to pieces. He did not want to copy: he wanted to understand.

An indication of how his mind was working during these years may be seen in the beautiful portrait of a mistress of Lodovico Sforza, painted soon after Leonardo arrived in Milan. The sitter, who could have been no more than a girl when he painted her, was probably Cecilia Gallerani. The ermine which she holds in her arms was an emblem of Lodovico, and is probably also a pun on the girl's name. And in a sense the whole picture is a pun, for Leonardo has matched the ermine in the girl. In the skull under the long brow, in the lucid eyes, in the stately, beautiful, stupid head of the girl, he has rediscovered the animal nature; and done so without malice, almost as a matter of fact. The very carriage of the girl and the ermine, the gesture of the hand and the claw, explore the character with the anatomy. The painting is as much a research into man and animal, and a creation of unity, as is Darwin's *Origin of Species*.

The notebooks of Leonardo are as unexpected, and as personal, as everything about him. There are about five thousand pages of them which have been preserved. Each page is a wonderful jumble of drawings and notes, in which a piece of geometry, a horse's head, an astronomical conjecture, and a flower stand side by side. A photograph shows all this with Leonardo's transparent clarity, but it does not show the delicate scale on which Leonardo worked. Many of the pages in the notebooks, crowded with detail, are no bigger than a man's hand. This is perhaps another expression of Leonardo's withdrawn and indrawn character, and so, no doubt, is the mirror writing which Leonardo used, writing with his left hand. The shading in his drawings is left-handed also, but it is not certain that he painted with his left hand. It is possible that he had damaged his right hand in Florence, and that thereafter he still used it, but only for the most delicate parts of his pictures. The pocket notebooks, the left-handed shading, the mirror writing, express something else, too, in Leonardo's character: a determination to do everything for himself, in his own way, down to the smallest detail. Witness, for example, his anatomical drawings showing the hollows and blood vessels in the head—drawings so exact that they have been compared point by point with photographs made by X-ray or by radioactive tracers. It is not only the enormous scope of his researches that is impressive, it is the absorption, the meticulousness, and the intensity with which he looked for the mechanism behind what he saw. Leonardo was not merely an original man, in the sense that he had two or three profound and new ideas. He had a passion for looking afresh at everything that came into his life, no matter how trivial the occasion. In this sense, he was not merely an original but a perverse man; and perhaps all the oddities of his life reach back into the childhood of the lonely boy.

"Intellectual passion drives out sensuality," Leonardo wrote on a page of his notebooks. But perhaps his tragic and unfulfilled life proves that when the intellect becomes the subject of such a passion, it ends by being a kind of perversion.

Leonardo's notebooks from this time are full of the penetrating observation of nature, particularly in the anatomical drawings; and are full, too, of a springing invention which was fired by his observation. He had long been absorbed by the flight of birds, and now it led him to invent a parachute and a form of helicopter. The fact that the latter did not work may be blamed on the age in which he lived, which did not understand, and could not have commanded, the mechanical energy necessary for flight. He observed, one hundred years before Galileo, that the pendulum might be used to make a clockwork keep equal time. He saw that red light penetrates through mist and that blue light does not, and so devised practical rules for giving depth to the painting of landscapes. There are mechanisms on his pages here and there which he noted from others, but the bulk of what he outlined was original, and it included various types of bridges, a mechanical excavator, machines for grinding needles and mirrors, a rolling mill, an automatic file cutter, an instrument for measuring wind speeds, and a self-centering chuck. Here is a characteristic invention, which characteristically goes into every essential detail:

*A Way of Saving Oneself in a Tempest or
Shipwreck at Sea*

It is necessary to have a coat made of leather with a double hem over the breast of the width of a finger, and double also from the girdle to the knee, and let the leather of which it is made be quite air-tight. And when you are obliged to jump into the sea, blow out the lappets of the coat through the hems of the breast, and then jump into the sea. And let yourself be carried by the waves, if

there is no shore near at hand and you do not know the sea. And
always keep in your mouth the end of the tube through which the
air passes into the garment; and if once or twice it should become
necessary for you to take a breath when the foam prevents you,
draw it through the mouth of the tube from the air within the coat.

There is no wonder that, as Leonardo grew more absorbed in
the mechanism of nature, the work which he had come to Milan
to do was put off further and further. At last, in 1493, it could
be put off no longer. Lodovico Sforza was arranging to marry
his niece to the Emperor Maximilian. Leonardo made a full-sized
model of the statue of Francesco Sforza on horseback in clay. The
bronze to cast the statue was gathered, too, but that had to be
sent off next year to make cannon for Lodovico's allies. Lodovico
was now deep in intrigue, trying to marshal one group of the
city-states of Italy against another. Finally he invited the French
to come into Italy on his side, and they, as treacherous as Lodovico, entered Milan in 1499. Lodovico fled, but a year later they
took him prisoner.

Leonardo also fled from Milan in that year, a defeated man
now nearing fifty, who had given the richest years of his life to a
second-rate tyrant with a passion for power. The French archers
had used the clay horse and its rider as a target, and there remained
in Milan little to show for Leonardo's spent years except a painting of the Last Supper which began to molder on its damp convent
wall even before the artist died. The prior had complained that
Leonardo had been dilatory in finishing even that, and Leonardo
in revenge had said that he would paint the prior for eternity into
the figure of Judas. Yet, characteristically, when it came to the
point, Leonardo had done something more profound with the
figure of Judas: he had moved Judas out of the place that the
Middle Ages had assigned to him and had put him on the same
side of the table with Jesus.

Leonardo lived for twenty years after the fall of Milan, wandering irresolutely from one city to another, and from one commission
to another, without ever again settling down to any one. In 1502 he
served briefly in the train of Cesare Borgia as military engineer.

This was the same treacherous campaign on which Niccolò Machiavelli was present—the one which provided the Florentine diplomat with a portrait of undeviating ambition for *The Prince*.

Soon after, Florence commissioned two patriotic pictures of battle scenes, one from Leonardo and one from Michelangelo. Leonardo's drafts of the picture survive, but the painting itself deteriorated almost immediately. During this time Leonardo painted a portrait of the third wife of a local merchant named Giocondo. This is the *Mona Lisa*, which in its day was admired for the warmth of its flesh tones, and which time and varnish have now turned to the faint green of ice in a landscape of rocks.

Leonardo went back to Milan from time to time to make sketches, now, for another horse and rider. This time the rider was to be Gian Giacomo Trivulzio, the Italian condottiere who had fought on the side of the French in the battle for Milan and had overthrown his one-time master and Leonardo's patron, Lodovico. Once again, nothing came of this monument. Then, in 1513, the son of Lorenzo de' Medici became Pope Leo X, and Leonardo went to Rome, where Raphael and Michelangelo had been working for some years, and there received several papal commissions. The story goes that Leonardo began, upon his arrival, to make the varnish for one picture before he started to paint it, and that Leo X observed, sadly and wisely, "This man will never do anything, for he begins to think of the end before the beginning."

The King of France at last offered Leonardo a retreat without obligation near Amboise, and there he spent the remainder of his life, from 1516 until 1519. His self-portrait, drawn a few years earlier, shows him as a man looking much older than his sixty years, full-bearded and patriarchal, his eyes veiled against emotion and his mouth set bitterly, and the distress of an old age full of regrets for the wonderful things that he had planned and never finished now fills his notebooks. Once he had been so sure of his own gifts that there had seemed to be an infinity of time in which to fulfill them. In those confident young days he had written:

I wish to work miracles;—I may have less than other men who are more tranquil, or than those who aim at growing rich in a day.

Now he was conscious everyday of the merciless erosion of time, which leaves nothing of the living vigor and beauty of a man if the man has not perpetuated them in his own creations. Leonardo is looking into his own face when he thinks of Helen of Troy and, borrowing from Ovid, writes:

O Time, thou that consumest all things! O envious age, thou destroyest all things and devourest all things with the hard teeth of the years, little by little, in slow death! Helen, when she looked in her mirror and saw the withered wrinkles which old age had made in her face, wept, and wondered to herself why ever she had twice been carried away. O Time, thou that consumest all things! O envious age, whereby all things are consumed!

The works of art that Leonardo left behind are indeed sadly few —not a whole statue, about a dozen finished paintings, some fine anatomical and mechanical drawings, and otherwise only the thousands of sketches. For some artists with one small gift, this might be enough; but when we consider the prodigious talent of Leonardo, the instant eye, the exact hand, and the penetrating mind, we understand why he scribbled desperately on page after page of his later notebooks: "Tell me if anything at all was done . . . Tell me if anything at all was done . . ."

And no doubt Leonardo was right to think that he had wasted his life; but he was wrong to think that he had wasted his gifts. At bottom, his true gifts were not those of a painter, for his painting, original as it was, was not out of the reach of his contemporaries. As a painter Leonardo was in the stream of the Renaissance tradition which Botticelli, Raphael, Michelangelo, and others were also helping to form. Leonardo's most profound gifts were of another kind, and make him seem modern to us today, five hundred years after he lived.

The first of the gifts which made Leonardo a pioneer was his absorbed interest in the structure and mechanism of nature. The science of his day has hardly a hint of this because it was still dominated by a magical view of man. The alchemists of Leonardo's time believed that they would command nature only by breaking the natural order of things, by casting a spell over nature which made her function in a way contrary to her own laws. They wanted to bewitch the world, and to gain power by forcing it to obey them instead of the laws of nature. Leonardo realized, as his contemporaries did not, that we command nature only when we understand her, when we enter into her processes and give them scope to work naturally. He was full of contempt for those who wanted to force nature to do the impossible: "O speculators about perpetual motion, how many vain chimeras have you created in the like quest? Go and take your place with the seekers after gold."

Leonardo's second pioneering gift was to see that the structure of nature also reveals her processes, which are perpetually in movement and in development. The way a skeleton is hinged, the way a muscle is anchored, the way a leaf is veined—all such knowledge tells something about the functioning of the organism and therefore, in the end, about the whole cycle of its growth. Leonardo dismissed the easy appeals to vital forces and the spirits that inhabit living things with which his age fobbed off all questions; he looked for the strict mechanism by which living things move and act; and he saw that mechanism as something dynamic. This dynamic quality is present even in his simplest sketch of a machine, and in his old age it expressed itself in a growing preoccupation with the forms of plants and of flowing water. Leonardo did not think that a scientific analysis of the processes of nature deprived them of life; on the contrary, he wanted the analysis to express their changing and living movement.

Third, and most important, Leonardo understood that science is not a grand parade of a few cosmic theories, of the kind that Aristotle and Saint Thomas Aquinas had propounded. Until Leonardo's time a theory was expected to give a general explanation of some large phenomenon, such as the motion of the moon, and no one then asked whether the theory could also be made to match the precise times at which the moon rises and sets. The detail was not thought important, and any discrepancy between theory and fact was shrugged off as a point of detail. Leonardo for the first time elevated the detail so that it became once and for all the crucial test of a scientific theory. He was seldom misled by what the classical medicine of Galen said in general about the functioning of the heart or the way that the eye sees; he drew what his dissection showed him, and then asked how it could be squared with the vague medical beliefs which were then accepted.

Here we are at the center of Leonardo's pioneering mind. Because he had an exact eye, because he was a painter for whom nature lived not in generalities but in the very shape of a flower or a waterfall, he was at the opposite pole from theorizing scientists of his own age. Leonardo did not therefore lose interest in science: he transformed it. Only a painter could have forced science to change its outlook, and to become as dedicated as his art was to the discovery of the natural order in the minute detail of its structure. Leonardo *was* that painter, who is the true pioneer of science as we practice it.

His interest in what was new made him unwilling to look back; his gaze was outward and forward into nature. His passion for the exact turned him toward mathematics, his passion for the actual urged him to experiment, and it is significant that these two dominant themes—logic and experimentation—have remained, ever since Leonardo's time, at the base of scientific method.

It was natural that, with these gifts, Leonardo should have quarreled with the classical and literary Renaissance in which he was brought up and should have turned to a more popular and naturalistic Renaissance. It was natural that he should give up pictures for machines, and that his machines should have that subtle quality of human intelligence, of one operation controlling another, which today we call automation. It was natural that these interests should take him from the rich merchant culture of Florence to the brutal thrust for power of the Sforza and the Borgia. And it was natural and inevitable that a life at the courts of such men should have about it the modern ring of our own age, the pointless planning of pageants and machines of war, the aimless postponement of every constructive scheme, and the final despair of a great mind that from childhood has been baffled by an alien world. At the end of his life Leonardo wrote constantly of his visions of the cruelty of man to man, and what he foresaw links his gangster age to ours:

Of the Cruelty of Man

Creatures shall be seen upon the earth who will always be fighting one with another with very great losses and frequent deaths on either side. These shall set no bounds to their malice; by their fierce limbs a great number of the trees in the immense forests of the world shall be laid level with the ground; and when they have crammed themselves with food it shall gratify their desire to deal out death, affliction, labors, terrors, and banishment to every living thing. And by reason of their boundless pride they shall wish to rise towards heaven, but the excessive weight of their limbs shall hold them down. There shall be nothing remaining on the earth or under the earth or in the waters that shall not be pursued and molested and destroyed, and that which is in one country taken away to another; and their own bodies shall be made the tomb and the means of transit of all the living bodies which they have slain. O Earth! what delays thee to open and hurl them headlong into the deep fissures of thy huge abysses and caverns, and no longer to display in the sight of heaven so savage and ruthless a monster?

VI.

Pope Pius II

by IRIS ORIGO

The road that winds up from the eleventh-century *pieve* of Corsignano—roughhewn in the golden stone of the region and contain-
ing the font in which Aeneas Silvius Piccolomini was christened—
to the perfect little Renaissance city of Pienza—named after Pope
Pius II—is a short one. But the ascent it symbolizes was one
unusually swift and high even in a period in which able men
quickly made their mark—the ascent which led a clever country
boy from a humble secretary's desk to Peter's throne. A shrewd
statesman, an elegant humanist, an inquiring traveler—keenly
addicted to the learning of the past, but equally alive to any
new ideas of discoveries of his own time—witty and urbane,
skeptical and adaptable, he might be considered an entirely typical
figure of the Renaissance, had he not, at the very summit of his
career, devoted his last years to a vast and impracticable idea
which was more closely in harmony with the spirit of an earlier
age: the last Crusade. To carry out this plan, he cast aside every
obstacle suggested by expediency or prudence and certainly
hastened, though well knowing that his scheme had failed, his
own death.

Aeneas Silvius Piccolomini, the son of an impoverished country nobleman who had been a soldier of fortune, was born in 1405 in the little Tuscan village of Corsignamo, on the bare, dust-colored hills of the Val d'Orcia. A clever boy, he was sent by his father at the age of eighteen to Siena, the city which he called "sacred to Venus." There, while certainly not neglecting the charms of the beautiful Sienese women, he ardently pursued his legal studies with the celebrated jurist Sozzini, and later on continued his classical studies in Florence with Filelfo. Too poor to buy all the books he needed, he would sit up at night copying out long passages from the volumes lent to him by his friends—once even setting his nightcap on fire, as he nodded over his work. Cicero, Virgil, Livy, these were his first models, and among the moderns, when first he began to write verse, Petrarch. His first glimpse of the efficacy of eloquence, when he saw the whole congregation of Siena swept off their feet by the sermons of the famous popular preacher Saint Bernardino, excited him so much that he pursued him to Rome, to ask whether he, too, should not follow the same path. But Saint Bernadino firmly dissuaded him, telling the future Pope to return to the worldly pursuits for which he was apparently more fitted.

It was thus not as a priest but merely as a young scholar with some legal training that Aeneas' career began. Cardinal Capranica, passing through Siena on his way to Basle to claim redress from the Ecumenical Council in his quarrel with Pope Eugenius IV, took him with him as his secretary—and in Basle the young man at once found ample scope for his talents. The Council—which had recently reaffirmed its supremacy even over the Pope, and which had the support of both the King of France and the Emperor Sigismund—was confronting two vast tasks, the destruction of heresy and the reformation of the Church. There Aeneas made the acquaintance of most of the great European prelates and observed their intrigues and counterintrigues; he fostered the cynical detachment already inherent in his Tuscan blood; and he acquired the adaptability, the breadth of vision, and the persuasive eloquence which were to lead him to success. In his *Commentaries* he related, with disarming vanity, that he once held his audience so riveted by his words that for two hours no one even spat!

For twenty years he led a wandering life between Switzerland, Germany, and Austria. He was sent on missions all over Europe: to James I of Scotland—probably for the purpose of inciting fresh border-raids against England—to the Hussite heretics of Bohemia, and to the hermit-duke Amedeus of Savoy, whom he described as leading, in his luxurious hermitage on the Lake of Geneva, "a life of pleasure rather than of penitence." He became known in Germany as "the apostle of humanism." He accepted a post in the chancery of Frederick III, negotiated the marriage of the young Emperor to Eleonora of Portugal, and later went to meet the young bride and to escort her and her bridegroom to Rome. Ambition, he quite frankly admitted, was to his mind the chief spur to every human activity. But he also found time to make love to many pretty women (declaring chastity to be a philosopher's virtue, not a poet's and sending home one of his bastards to be brought up by his father at Corsignano, "so that another little Aeneas may climb on your and my mother's knees") and to write some scurrilous tales and a little satirical treatise on the miseries of life at court, as well as the poems which caused him to be crowned as poet by the Emperor. To all this he added a formidable list of more serious works, which included treatises on education, on rhetoric, on the Holy Roman Empire, and even on horses; histories of Bohemia, of the Goths, of the Council of Basle, of the Diet of Ratisbon, and of the Emperor Frederick III; and some *Lives of Illustrious Men*—and finally, after becoming Pope, the famous *Commentaries*.

It was not until the age of forty that he returned to Rome, obtained the forgiveness of Pope Eugenius IV, and conducted the negotiations which led to the reconciliation of the Papacy with the Empire—and it was only two years later, in 1447, that he at last took orders. After this, the speed of his preferment was remarkable. Within a year he became Bishop of Trieste and resumed his travels between Italy, Austria, and Bohemia; in 1449 he was made Bishop of Siena; in 1456 Calixtus III nominated him Cardinal of St. Sabina; and two years later, in 1458, he was elected Pope.

Success comes most swiftly and completely not to the greatest or perhaps even to the ablest men, but to those whose gifts are most completely in harmony with the taste of their times. The Renaissance man admired versatility, scholarship, eloqence, diplomacy, and an inquiring and balanced mind; above all, he valued style, both in life and letters. All these were qualities possessed by the new Pope to a very high degree. *"Aenaem rejicite, Pium suscipite"* (Reject Aeneas and accept Pius), he wrote, with a harking-back to the Virgilian phrase which had also determined the choice of his new name—and it is certainly true that he abstained for good, after his ordination, from the loose living and scurrilous writings of his early years, and lived a life of great industry, sobriety, and benevolence. "I do not deny my past," he wrote to his friend John Freund, "but we are old, nearer to death . . . I have been a great wanderer from what is right, but I know it, and I hope the knowledge has not come too late."

He was not exempt from one fault of many other pontiffs: nepotism. Three members of his household (including his nephew Francesco) were given the cardinal's hat at the same consistory, another nephew, Antonio Piccolomini, was made commander of Castel Sant' Angelo, and his sisters were richly endowed with both money and palaces.

The fullest picture of his daily activities is to be found in the book which was the mirror of his times and of himself: his *Commentaries.* This is not only one of the most readable autobiographies ever written, but also a historical record of many of the important events of Pius' time, seen with a sharp eye and a ripe judgment, and enlivened by brilliant sketches of men and places, and by perceptive reflections on human nature. *"Nil habuit ficti, nil simulati"*—nothing was there in him of deceit or pretense, wrote one of his earliest biographers—and indeed this book carried these qualities so far that when it was first published in 1584 (during the Counter Reformation), it was thought necessary not only to prune it severely, but even to ascribe its authorship to its copyist, Gobellinus of Bonn, so that "matters which the heretics gladly seize upon" should not come from a pope's pen. Now that the full text is again available, however, we are afforded an unvarnished picture of the Pope's contemporaries. It is not always flattering. He described the Florentines as "traders, a sordid populace who can be persuaded to nothing noble." "When once Pius asked the Bishop of Orta what he thought of Florence and he replied that it was a pity that so beautiful a woman had not a husband, the Pope replied, 'She lacks a husband, but not a lover.' As though to say she had no king, but a tyrant, meaning Cosimo." Of the Bolognese he wrote: "They are cruel rather than brave at home, while abroad they are known to be cowards," and many pages were filled with attacks on the Venetians, who drew back from their promises of alliance against the Turks, while he said, "They favored the war against the Turks with their lips but condemned it in their hearts." "Glorious deeds," the Pope said, "are not embraced by democracies, least of all by merchants, who, being by their nature intent on profit, loathe those splendid things that cannot be achieved without expense."

The tyrants of the Italian states were described with an equally sharp pen. Cosimo de' Medici, indeed, was admitted to be "more lettered than merchants are wont to be," but Borso d'Este was depicted as "listening to himself when speaking, as though he pleased himself better than he did others," and as a man "whose mouth was full of flattery mixed with lies." And Sigismondo Malatesta, for all his brilliance of mind, artistic sensibility, and military skill, was described as "a man essentially pagan" and "so avaricious that he never shrank not only from looting but from theft, so ruled by his passions that he raped his daughters and his sons-in-law. He surpassed all barbarians in cruelty." The Pope publicly declared that, just as some holy men are canonized, so Sigismondo should be "enrolled as a citizen of Hell." On the steps of St. Peter's his effigy was burned, bearing the inscription: "Sigismondo Malatesta, son of Pandolfo, king of traitors, hated by God and man, condemned to the flames by the vote of the Holy Senate."

It is when he is writing of the members of his own Curia, however, that Pius II's indictments are most startling. Shortly before his death he addressed a secret consistory of his cardinals: "Like businessmen who have failed to pay their creditors, we have no credit left. The priesthood is an object of scorn. They say we live for pleasure, hoard up money, serve ambition, sit on mules or pedigree horses, spread out the fringes of our cloaks and go about the city with fat cheeks under our red hats and ample hoods, that we breed dogs for hunting, spend freely upon players and parasites, but nothing in defense of the Faith. Nor is it all a lie!"

Yet when Pius met true saintliness or valor, he was swift to recognize it. It was he who canonized Saint Catherine of Siena and who, in describing the entry into Vienna of the humble Franciscan friar Giovanni da Capistrano—"with so tiny a body, so advanced in years, so dried up, exhausted, all skin and nerves and yet always serene"—at once recognized in him the attributes of a saint. He also gave a singularly detached and impartial account of the story of Joan of Arc, "that astonishing and marvelous maid," ending with the comment, "Whether her career was the work of God or a human invention we would not like to say."

But where his regard was not awakened, no figure was so eminent as to escape his darts. He described James I of Scotland as "smallish, hot-tempered, and greedy for vengeance," and said of his former master, the antipope Felix V, that when he appeared without his beard, he looked like "an unsightly monkey." Before the assembled Curia he referred to the Cardinal of San Marco as "the buffoon of your Order," and to the brilliant, unscrupulous French Cardinal d'Estouteville of Rouen as "a slippery fellow who would sell his own soul." And here is his account of another prelate, Jouffroy, Cardinal of Aras—a man "made mad by too much learning"—"He wanted to seem devout and would say Mass, sometimes in the Basilica of St. Peter's, and sometimes elsewhere. By face and gesture he would show how much he was carried away, drawing sighs from the bottom of his chest, weeping and, as it were, conversing with God. But before he had taken off his sacred vestments and left the altar he had cuffed one or another of his servants who had made some slight mistake in his ministration . . ."

His description, too, of the conclave by which he himself was elected Pope is as cynical as it is convincing. "The men having most power in the College . . . summoned the others and demanded the Apostolate for themselves or for their friends. They implored, promised, threatened; some, even, without a blush and forgetting all modesty, spoke in praise of themselves . . ." Aeneas' chief rival was the Cardinal of Rouen, and many were the intrigues which took place in the latrines of the Vatican ("as being a private hiding place"). The French Cardinal openly distributed promises of honors and posts to those whose support he thought he could obtain, but the next morning Aeneas called in turn upon *his* friends—appealing to the loyalty of one prelate and the vanity or self-interest of another. In the end nine votes for him and six for the Cardinal of Rouen were dropped into the golden chalice. But still the required majority had not been obtained. "All sat in their places, silent, pale, as though they had been struck senseless. No one spoke for some time, no one opened his mouth, no one moved any part of his body, except the eyes, which turned this way or that. The silence was astonishing, astonishing, too, the appearance of those men, as though you had found yourself among their statues . . . Then the Vice-Chancellor Rodrigo [the future Pope Alexander VI] rose and said, 'I accede to the Cardinal of Siena!' And his words were like a sword through Rouen's heart . . ." Another followed him, but still one vote was lacking, that of the old, fat Cardinal Prospero Colonna. As he rose he was seized by each arm by the cardinals of Nicaea and Rouen, who tried to hustle him out of the room. But before they could do so, he shouted, "I too, accede to Siena, and I make him Pope!"

Pius II's *Commentaries,* however, will not now be read chiefly for their account of the intrigues of the Curia or the politics of the Italian states. What gives them their peculiar flavor is their revelation of the point of view of a Renaissance man. "My spirit is an inquiring one," Aeneas wrote of himself in his youth, and in this he never changed. As an antiquarian, his curiosity embraced Christian and pagan monuments alike. In England he admired the stained-glass windows of York Cathedral and the shrine of Saint

Thomas à Becket in Canterbury, "at which it is a crime to offer any metal less than silver," but he was no less interested in the translation of Thucydides in St. Paul's Cathedral, and in being told that Newcastle was founded by Julius Caesar. In Hadrian's Villa he tried to reconstruct the origins of the ruins. On his visit to Federigo da Montefeltro, the Pope and condottiere discussed not the politics of the day, but the arms used in the Trojan War. On his way to the Congress of Mantua he turned aside to search for the labyrinth of Clusium described by Pliny, and visited the house called Virgil's Villa. Even in his last years, crippled with gout, he was carried in his litter to Tusculum, Tibur, and Falerii; he examined "with great pleasure" the Roman ship recently dug up in the Lake of Nemi, and rowed down the Tiber to Ostia, speculating about the Latin name of the fine sturgeons he was given, and the site of one of the Roman palaces. At Albano he visited the old monastery of San Paolo, which its new owner, the Cardinal of Aquileia, had transformed into a fine villa surrounded by gardens, and the deserted church belonging to the Cardinal de Foix, which was "without roof, altar, or doors" and served only as a stable for cattle and goats. "These," he dryly commented, "are the Canons appointed by the Cardinal of Albano to perform God's service day and night." With regard to the preservation of ancient monuments, however, his own conduct was somewhat inconsistent. When, on the Appian way, he found a man digging up some stones of the Roman pavement, he sharply rebuked him, bidding Prince Colonna never again to allow the public road to be touched, and he even issued a Bull forbidding the use of ancient columns and statues for making mortar. But he himself used, to build the Loggia della Benedizione and the marble steps leading up to St. Peter's, many fragments from the Colosseum, the Forum, or the Baths of Caracalla, and he constructed most of the great new fortress at Tivoli with material from the amphitheater of that city.

He was in some ways singularly free from the superstitious beliefs of his time, rebuking Borso d'Este for "heeding the pagan folly" of his astrologers, and refusing, even after being racked with fever for seventy-five days, to summon a magician who was "said to have cured of fever two thousand men in the camp of Niccolò Piccinino." But he told a Saxon student who asked him whether he knew of a Mount of Venus in Italy, in which the magic arts were taught, that "in Umbria . . . near the town of Nursia [Norcia], there is a cave beneath a sharp rock, in which water flows. There, as I remember to have heard, are witches, demons, and dark shades, and the man who is brave enough can see and speak to the ghosts and learn the magic arts."

In his travels he always investigated eagerly, if skeptically, any local legend or tradition. In Scotland he was fascinated by the legend of the Barnacle Geese, which told "of a tree growing on a river bank, whose fruit rotted if it fell to the ground, but if it fell into water, it came to life and turned into birds; but when he [Piccolomini] went thither and made inquiries, eager for a miracle, he found that it was a lie . . ." When he visited the slopes of Monte Amiata, he looked for the herb called Carolina because, according to tradition "it was once revealed by God to Charlemagne as a cure for the plague" and he succeeded in finding it—"a herb with prickly leaves which cling to the ground and are set around a flower similar to that of a thistle." He added, however, "Pius considered it a fable invented by Charlemagne's admirers."

He had an observant eye, too, for the different sorts of men and manners that he met upon his travels. In Scotland—where he spent one night in a rough farmhouse, with the goats picking the straw out of his pallet—he observed with interest that the white bread and wine that he had with him were such rarities that "pregnant women and their husbands drew near to the table, fingering the bread, sniffing the wine, and asking for a taste." He noticed, too, that "nothing gives the Scots more pleasure than to hear the English abused." In Basle he was impressed by the well-built stone houses and well-kept gardens, with fountains "as numerous as those of Viterbo," and in Vienna—according to his *Life of Frederick III*—by the comfortable dining halls with stoves and glass windows, where songbirds were kept, as well as by the fine churches and spacious cellars. He even described a convent for the redemption of penitent prostitutes, "who sing hymns in the Teutonic language day and night . . . But if one of them is caught singing again, she is cast into the Danube." But he also complained of the rough German table manners, of a court in which any falconer or stableboy was more welcome than a scholar, and above all, of the gross drunkenness. He described how Heinrich, Count of Gorizia, would wake up his two little boys by a virtuous Hungarian lady in the middle of the night to pour wine down their throats. When the sleepy children spat it out, he turned upon his wife shouting, "Strumpet, these brats are none of mine!"

Perhaps the most delightful passages in the *Commentaries,* as in Pius' letters, are those which reflect his passion for natural beauty. He might, indeed, be considered, with Petrarch, the first of the Romantic travelers. At Viterbo he went out almost every day at dawn "to enjoy the sweet air before it grows hot and to gaze at the blossoming sky-blue flax." At Bolsena he insisted on being rowed out to the islands in the lake, and whenever possible, he preferred to hold his consistories out of doors, especially in the great beech woods of Monte Amiata, "beneath this tree or that, and also by the sweetly running stream . . . Sometimes it happened that as the Pope was signing documents the dogs flung themselves upon some huge stag hiding nearby, which would drive them back with its horns or its hoofs and make off with all speed for the mountains." Often, too, he picnicked with his Curia in a meadow or poplar grove—though whether his cardinals, mostly elderly and urban gentlemen, enjoyed this habit is not related. One evening, as the Pope was returning home through some meadows, a cowherd, "seeing the golden litter carried by its porters and surrounded by horsemen . . . milked a cow that was near him and, full of joy, offered to the Pope the bowl which he used for eating and drinking, filled to the brim with milk . . . Pope Pius . . . was not too proud to put his lips to the black and greasy bowl."

One of Pius' most endearing traits was his simple enjoyment of homely pleasures: the cheese of Monte Oliveto, "which Tuscans consider the best in the world," the fresh trout which he saw caught on the Monte Amiata, and the engaging antics of his sister's baby. He even devoted a whole page to the misadventures of his poor little puppy, Musetta, who first fell into a cistern full of water and, when rescued at the last gasp, "was taken to the Pope, to whom she continued to whimper for a long time as if she wanted to tell him about her danger and stir his pity," but then was bitten by a large monkey, and finally, having climbed up on a high window sill, was seized by a violent gust of wind and dashed upon the rocks. The Pope sadly commented that, like some men, she was plainly foredestined to a violent end.

He described with relish the horse and foot races in Pienza, where a small and beardless grown-up slave inserted himself among the boys and defeated a little boy from Pienza, "with fair hair and a beautiful body, though all bedaubed with mud, who . . . bewailed his fortune and cursed himself for not having run faster. His mother was there, a handsome woman, comforting her child with gentle words and wiping off his sweat with a towel." "The Pope and cardinals"—so ends this chapter—"watched from a high window with no small merriment, though in the intervals they were busy with affairs of state."

The occasion of these events was the inauguration of the cathedral and palace which the famous Florentine architect Bernardo Rossellino had built at Corsignano—now renamed Pienza— as a summer residence for the papal court. The little city is still as perfectly harmonious a work of art as the early Renaissance has produced—the cathedral being flanked on one side of a little paved square by the papal palace, and on the others by the episcopal palace and town hall. Some smaller palaces were built nearby for the cardinals and their courts. The cost, however, was so much higher than the original estimate that everyone expected the architect to be cast into prison. But the Pope, after inspecting the buildings, sent for him and said: "You did well, Bernardo, to lie to us about what this undertaking would cost us. Had you spoken the truth, you had never persuaded us to spend so much money, and this fair palace and this church, the loveliest in all Italy, would never have existed. . . . We thank you, and we consider you deserving of special honor." And he issued a Bull forbidding the defacing of any of the church's walls or pillars, the building of any other chapels or altars, or any other change that might mar the church's perfect symmetry. "If any do otherwise, may he be anathema and absolvable only by the authority of the Bishop of Rome, except in the hour of death."

This happy return to his native city was perhaps the last carefree incident of the Pope's life. His remaining years were obsessed by a single idea: the coercion of the reluctant princes of Christendom to fight against the Turks.

It is not difficult—even without attributing to Pius II the religious fervor of an Urban II or a Saint Catherine—to understand his motives. He was well aware of how closely Hungary and Austria, and beyond them Italy herself, were threatened by the rising ambition of that astute and designing sultan, Mohammed II. His historical imagination was intensely conscious of the ancient traditions of the Holy Roman Empire, and of the Papacy as the savior of Christendom. And as he himself would have been the first to admit, his sense of drama was fired by the image of himself as the central figure in the most significant of all wars, once again leading princes and peoples against the Crescent in the name of the Cross.

Long before his accession, Aeneas had tried to awaken the European princes to the Turkish menace. At the coronation of Frederick III he had pointed out that Hungary had become the last bulwark of Christianity, and when Constantinople fell he was among the first to realize that henceforth the doors of Europe would always remain open to the Turk. "I see faith and learning," he wrote, "destroyed together." Aeneas implored both the Emperor and the Pope, Nicholas V, to convoke a European congress at which the princes would agree to a truce with each other, "and turn their arms instead against the enemies of the Cross." A Diet was actually held at Ratisbon, at which the few delegates who came voted for the Crusade, but only a few months later, when another congress was held in Frankfurt, most of them had already changed their minds. "They would not listen to the names of Emperor or Pope, but said they were deceivers and greedy men, who wanted to make not war but money." Aeneas was still struggling to persuade them to confirm their promises, when the sudden death of the Pope "rent the web that had been so long in weaving."

Immediately after his accession Pius returned to the charge. He summoned another congress at Mantua and, though crippled by gout and suffering from stone and bronchitis, decided to attend it himself. "It is all-important," he had written, "that a war should begin well, for the end of a war is often implicit in its beginnings." Certainly the beginning of this one foreshadowed its failure. The Pope set forth for Mantua with most of his cardinals, but when he arrived there, he found himself almost alone. His court implored him to go home again. Had they been brought here, they asked, to discuss a Crusade with the Mantuan frogs? Messengers from Thomas Palaeologous of the Morea (the southern part of the Peloponnesus) brought desperate appeals for help, but there were few to listen to them. The Duke of Burgundy now said that he was too old to come. The King of France, exasperated by the Pope's recent support of the accession to the Kingdom of Naples of Ferrante of Aragon, sent word that he could join no Crusade so long as he was still at war with England. England—torn by the Wars of the Roses—sent a similar message. Frederick III was engaged in invading the Kingdom of Hungary, while the envoys of that country—which alone, in the recent past, had defended Europe against the Turks—bitterly complained of this new menace. No single voice was raised to echo the old Crusade cry: *"Deus lo vult*—it is God's will!" Of the Italian rulers, Borso d'Este declared that his astrologers forbade him to attend; Malatesta suggested the employment of Italian mercenaries, but only to get their pay for himself. The Florentines and Venetians both feared the loss of their eastern trade, but Venice promised to furnish sixty galleys, if every expense was paid from the general treasury and she was given the supreme command of the naval forces and awarded the spoils of the war. "To a Venetian," the Pope commented, "everything is just that is good for the State; everything pious that increases the Empire."

Yet when at last he was in the presence of those envoys who

did come, the Pope showed much of his old fire. He had learned to conceal his physical pain so well that it was only revealed by his yellow color and drawn features and by an occasional compression of his lips. The French, in return for their participation, demanded the re-establishment of the Angevin rule in Naples, and believed that the Pope's illness would at once cause him to yield. But he declared: "Though I should die in the middle of the assembly, yet shall I reply to that proud-stomached delegation!" Speaking with as much eloquence and energy as in his youth, his cough ceased, and the color returned to his old cheeks. Even his most bitter opponents admitted that he had "spoken like a Pope." Moreover, in an attempt to shame the princes into following his example, he declared that he himself would lead the Crusade. "We can be borne in Our litter to the camp." On January 14, 1460, the Holy War was formally declared, and, discouraged but not defeated, the Pope started on his long journey home.

Before actually embarking on the Crusade, however, Pius II made one last curious effort to come to terms with the infidel— one which, if successful, might well have changed the course of European history. In a long and eloquent letter he attempted to convert the Sultan Mohammed II to Christianity. If he accepted baptism, the Pope wrote, a second Roman Empire might arise in the East, with Mohammed at its head. Pius reminded the Sultan that Clovis had brought Christianity to the Franks, and Constantine to the Romans; he depicted a Europe once more united and, for the first time in centuries, at peace. The epistle—which now reads more like a fine literary exercise than a political document —was widely circulated in Europe, but whether it ever even reached the Sultan is not known. Certainly no reply was ever received in Rome.

It was now plain that the Turks could be conquered only by arms. In a last attempt to arouse the Roman people the Pope decided to display to them—in what Gregorovius calls "one of the curious scenes of the Roman Renaissance"—a singularly precious relic: the skull of the Apostle Andrew, which the exiled Despot of the Morea, Thomas Palaeologus, had brought to him—

"the symbol of the Empire of Constantine and Justinian, and of the Church of Origen and Photius." Three cardinals, who had gone to fetch the head at Narni, were met at the Ponte Molle by the Pope and the other cardinals, and after a solemn *Te Deum* they accompanied it in procession to St. Peter's. "It was a splendid spectacle," Pius wrote, "to see those old men walk on foot through the mud holding palms in their hands and wearing miters on their white heads . . . Some who till then had lived delicately and could hardly move a hundred paces except on horseback, on that day . . . walked two miles through mud and water with ease." All along the route, windows were hung with tapestries and lit up with torches and oil lamps; altars were set up at street corners, branches of fragrant shrubs were set alight. "Any man who possessed paintings or a fine and lifelike statue displayed them in the portico before his door." Little stages were set up, on which children, dressed as angels, sang or played musical instruments.

Finally, on reaching St. Peter's, the Pope stood at the top of the marble stair before the church and displayed the head to the assembled crowd, renewing his own vow to the Apostle "to recover thy sheep and thy dwelling-place on earth," and calling upon God to deliver Christendom from the Turks. "Then there arose a great sound, like the murmur of many waters."

In the following spring, since the Turkish army was engaged in Bosnia, the Venetians, who had concluded an alliance with Hungary, decided that the moment was propitious to send off their own fleet to the Peloponnesus. *"We* are already at war," they declared. Pius had no illusions about the Venetian motives, but, as he pointed out to the Florentine envoys, even though the Venetians were "seeking the Peloponnesus and not Jesus. . . . if Venice is victorious, the Church will be victorious. . . . This war is our common war." Moreover, at just this moment, a most fortunate event had come to strengthen the Pope's hand. In the wooded hills of Tolfa, which were within the Patrimony, some mines of alum, the precious dye until then imported from Turkey, were discovered. This Pius declared to be a miracle, and at once set aside all its profits for the Crusade. On October 22, 1463, he issued the Bull *Ezechielis,* repeating his determination to lead the troops of Christendom himself. "In our spirit, old as it is, and in our sick body there is a determination to make war upon the Turks."

Already, however, he realized that many of his allies had failed him—in particular Francesco Sforza of Milan, Louis XI of France, and his vassal the Duke of Burgundy. The Venetian troops in the Peloponnesus had been swiftly defeated by the Turks, and their commander killed. The only troops to reach Ancona were a handful of unscrupulous adventurers, greedy for gain and loot. The Archbishop of Crete was appointed to weed them out, rejecting all those who had neither arms nor money.

Nevertheless, on June 14, 1464, in a solemn ceremony at St. Peter's, the Pope took the Cross, and four days later, so ill that he had to be carried onto his barge, he set forth. Turning back at the Ponte Molle for a last glimpse of Rome, he bade his city farewell, declaring, "You will never see me alive again." In all the history of the Crusades there are few episodes more pathetic than this journey of the dying Pope up the Tiber and across the Apennines —well aware that his enterprise was doomed. Often, as they drew near the coast, his attendants would draw the curtains of his litter, so that he might not see the bands of deserters who, scenting the prospect of defeat, were fleeing home before they had even begun to fight.

When the Pope reached Ancona, no Venetian ship was to be seen, and day after day, from the windows of the bishop's palace at the summit of the town, Pius scanned the Adriatic in vain for the galleys of Saint Mark. The city was now short of food and water and a pestilence had broken out, and the Pope himself was wasting away with dysentery.

When at last, on August 12, the Doge Cristoforo Moro sailed in with twelve ships, Pius was too ill to receive him. "Until now," he said, "it was a fleet that was lacking. Now the fleet has come, but I shall not be there." Two days later, feeling his end to be near, he summoned to his bedside the prelates who had come to Ancona with him, gave them his blessing, and told them that he

was leaving them to finish what he had begun. Then, left alone
with his nephew, his secretary, and his old friend Cardinal Am-
manati, he once again exhorted the latter not to draw back. "Urge
my brothers to go on with the Crusade . . . Woe befall you if you
draw back from God's work." Asking for his friend's prayers, he
lay back and died before the dawn.

On the next day his body was carried to the cathedral, where
the Doge pronounced a long and insincere oration over it and
then at once set sail for Venice, while the cardinals hurried back
to Rome to elect a new pope. The last Crusade was over, with the
death of the only man who had believed in it.

VII.

Doge Francesco Foscari

by H. R. TREVOR-ROPER

In 1423 the old Doge of Venice, Tommaso Mocenigo, lay dying. The prosperity of the city was now at its height; this indeed was the golden age of the republic. But for a generation grave problems had clouded the city's future, threatening not only its security and its carefully nurtured wealth, but its very survival. Now it seemed at the parting of the ways: should it concentrate on its empire abroad or on its base at home? For both were threatened.

The empire abroad was centered in the Aegean Sea, although it extended to the factories in Constantinople and on the routes to the Middle and Far East. Here the threat came from the Ottoman Turks, now settled in Europe, with their capital at Adrianople, and pushing into the Balkans. All the efforts of Venice were needed to keep them out of the Aegean, and for years that had been the prime object of Venetian diplomacy.

The threat to the home base came from closer quarters: from new powers which were rising ominously in and around Italy. Hitherto, Venice had been able to build up its empire abroad because its neighbors at home had given little trouble. Bishoprics, communes, petty princes—they could not be ignored, but equally they offered no temptations compared with the huge profits of the

Levant. So the republic had practiced a policy of the balance of power, involving the minimum of direct intervention. But now these petty neighbors were becoming part or projections of greater powers, and these greater powers were threatening the very life of Venice. The rulers of Hungary and Naples were closing in on its Adriatic lifeline. Above all, a menacing new state was pressing down the valley of the Po. For this was the time when the free republics of Italy were gradually being converted into despotic princely states; and the greatest of these states was the new duchy of Milan, under the Visconti family. Having crushed the liberties of Milan, the Visconti were creating around it an even larger hinterland or *retroterra*. In the south they had absorbed the great mercantile republic of Genoa which, being confined between the Ligurian Alps and the sea, lacked such a *retroterra* in which to fight. In the east the Visconti were pushing toward another great mercantile republic, which was squeezed between the lagoons and the sea—Venice.

How could the republic ensure its survival? The answer, according to some Venetians, was to enlarge its own *retroterra,* the Venetian *terraferma*—a process which had already begun, with the annexation of Padua, Vicenza, and Verona. But there were others who distrusted this policy. Land wars, they said, were costly; they distracted the city from its real task, in the East; they created a new class of landed nobility and made the city dependent on condottieri; and was it not precisely out of the landed nobility and condottieri that the powerful new group of princes, which threatened the liberties of all Italian cities, was rising?

The Doge Mocenigo was one who argued thus. As he lay dying he summoned to his bed the ducal councilors and there delivered a famous speech. The war for the *terraferma*, he said, had shattered the finances of the republic. It could not be continued. The wealth of Venice lay in manufacture, trade, and shipping: only by keeping to these pursuits, and to peace, would the city master the wealth of Christendom. Therefore they must be careful to appoint a sound successor to himself. Then he went down the list of the possible candidates. Bembo, Loredan, Mocenigo,

Contarini—the political members of the great mercantile families who formed the closed aristocracy of Venice—there was something to be said for them all. But at the end he warned them explicitly against one man: Francesco Foscari, he said, was proud, ambitious, unscrupulous. If he were Doge, it would mean war, war, war . . .

To us there may seem something unbalanced in such a warning. Already by that time the republic had achieved its perfect aristocratic form—a form which was to be final (in all essentials) for centuries. Gone were the days when the people had power of election; since 1297 the Greater Council, the legislature and electorate of the republic, had been "closed"—that is, confined to the nobility, who in turn kept careful control over their own membership. Gone, too, were the days when the Doge, however elected, had exercised personal power. By now successive "ducal promises"—the conditions which the nobility, after observing the faults of each Doge, imposed upon his successor—had reduced the Doge to a mere figurehead. If offered the dogeship, a Venetian nobleman was unable by law to refuse it. Once elected, his power was narrowly circumscribed. He was unable to travel outside Venice. Neither he nor his sons could marry foreigners without permission. Neither his sons nor his personal officers could hold public positions under him (except as ambassadors or naval commanders, in which jobs they could not make trouble at home), and his official councilors, without whom he could do nothing, not even open a formal letter, could not be chosen by him. His income was fixed and his expenses limited, lest he should raise a party by bribery. His authority over the citizens was reduced, lest he should raise a mob in his support. He was not even allowed to give himself social airs. He could not set up his escutcheons in public places, nor answer to honorific titles. To foreigners, as representative of the greatest, richest republic in Italy, he might be *Serenissimo Principe;* at home, in that republic, he was only *Messer lo Doge.* And finally, he could not even lay down his office at will: except with the consent of his six councilors, ratified by the approval of the Greater Council, he could not even abdicate. Why then should an ambitious man want to be doge, and what could an ambitious man do, even if he were doge?

Nevertheless, Mocenigo's warning cannot have been entirely groundless. The Venetian constitution may have been completely aristocratic, and its aristocratic character may have been jealously preserved by a perpetual subdivision of authority, indirect elections, and a complex tissue of checks and balances. But even the most perfect constitution is operated by men with human passions, and the more complex a constitution is, the more certainly it falls into the hands of skillful politicians; and skilled politicians, even with the old rules, may play a new game. In the fifteenth century a new game was being played in all the republics of Italy. Faced by new problems, their old constitutions were crumbling, and new men—sometimes patricians rising out of their midst, sometimes condottieri in their service—were building up despotic rule. This had already happened in Milan, with the Visconti; it would happen again, with the Sforza. Soon it would happen in Florence, too. Cosimo de' Medici might begin as *pater patriae,* "the first citizen" of the republic. He would end by founding a dynasty that would last for centuries. Remembering this, no one can assume that even the Venetian constitution was proof against overthrow from above by an ambitious doge who, as a war leader, might build up a new form of patronage and power. Such at least may have been the fear which inspired the Doge Mocenigo to warn his fellow noblemen against electing, as his successor, Francesco Foscari.

Who was the man who aroused these fears? The great Venetian aristocrats are always somewhat impersonal figures. The very system, with its intense jealousy of individual power, tended to depersonalize them. For it was the essential character of the Venetian republic that all personality was ruthlessly subordinated to the state. Instead of the cutthroat private enterprise of Genoa, or the brilliant individualism of Florence, here we see only an impersonal state capitalism, an implacable reason of state, an official state culture entirely hostile to "the cult of personality." So the official records of Venice do not bring to life even a controversial personality like Foscari. And yet he certainly was a controversial character. His whole reign shows it—a fact which is demonstrated, first of all, by the battle over his election.

Foscari, it is clear, was determined to be doge. Moreover, from the point of view of Mocenigo and his friends, he was an outsider. That was why they so feared him. He was also young (at fifty he was the youngest of the candidates); he was regarded as poor by the great "nabob" families, although he had enriched himself by marriage; he was experienced (after sharing his father's exile in Egypt, he had held most of the great elective offices of the state); and above all—and this was what Venice particularly distrusted—he was ambitious and the head of a party. Moreover, this party was particularly suspicious to the great mercantile aristocracy, like the Mocenigo, that customarily ruled Venice, for it was a party of "the poor nobles," the lesser noblemen, the radicals, the "Westerners" who favored war by land—as distinct from the "Easterners" with their Levantine interests. We are told that, as Procurator of St. Mark's, Foscari had used the large cash balances in his hands to create his following; he had relieved the wants of poor noblemen, given portions to their daughters, and made himself dangerous by their support. No doubt he had won other support by his merits, too. And finally, as was soon to be shown, he was a consummate election manager.

When the forty-one electors met, Foscari was not the favorite. He was too impulsive, too controversial, too committed to a policy. The favorite was Pietro Loredan, the admiral of the republic, who was also determined on office. But Loredan made the mistake of speaking confidently on his own behalf, which lost him votes. Foscari was much more prudent. Although his rivals did not know it, he had already nine ballots safely in his pocket. These voters acted as a bloc, but they did not reveal themselves until they had quietly contributed to the defeat of all the other candidates. Instead, they allowed it to appear that they, too, were opposed to Foscari. Then, suddenly, at the tenth ballot, they all plumped for the outsider and carried him into the ducal chair.

Thus began the longest ducal reign in the long history of the

Venetian republic. Foscari, who always liked panache, hastened to celebrate his victory. For a whole year he dazzled the city with feasts and pageants. The new Sala del Maggior Consiglio—the Hall of the Great Council—was opened with splendid ceremony. He fetched his wife, the Dogaressa, in triumph to the Palace in the ducal galley, the *Bucentaur,* attended by the noblewomen of Venice. These spectacles, incidentally, were something of a sop to the non-noble citizens of Venice who in that year lost their last vestigial rights in the government of the republic; but it is doubtful if their personal emphasis pleased the aristocracy. Then the Doge settled down to the business of government.

The character of Foscari's reign can be described in three words —pageantry, war, and dissention. There were feasts and spectacles of unexampled magnificence. There was also—as Mocenigo had prophesied—constant war for the *terraferma.* And thirdly, there was the undying jealousy and hatred of those whom Foscari had defeated—particularly of the Loredan family, whom he had pipped to the post. The pageantry gave his reign its outward splendor; the war its real content; and the hatred of the Loredan brought it to a tragic end.

The outward splendor was shown in many ways. New places, public and private, rose by the Grand Canal and the lagoon. The Rialto bridge was rebuilt. Paolo Uccello worked on mosaics in St. Mark's, Antonio Vivarini painted in San Pantaleon. Famous visitors were received with ever greater pomp and show. In 1428 it was the Prince of Portugal whom the *Bucentaur,* escorted by a fleet of boats, fetched in to a banquet attended by two hundred and fifty ladies dressed in cloth of gold and silk and jewels. In 1438 the Emperor of Byzantium himself, in his great time of trial with the Turks, condescended to come in person to Italy, with his brother the Despot of the Morea and the Patriarch of Constantinople, ready to accept the supremacy of the Roman Church in return for Western aid. When the *Bucentaur,* covered with red silk and golden emblems, carried the imperial party from the Lido, the whole lagoon was full of boats, flying banners and playing music, with oarsmen clad in cloth of gold. In 1452 even this event was eclipsed when the Holy Roman Emperor followed the Emperor of the East to Venice, and was drawn in triumph by the *Bucentaur* and the gaily colored boats up to the Grand Canal. By the next year the last Emperor of the East had perished in the sack of his capital, and the Doge Foscari would receive in Venice the fugitive scholars and salvaged treasures of Byzantium.

In Byzantine eyes, the fall of Byzantium was due to Venetian indifference. All through the reign of Foscari, it was said, the military resources of Venice had been turned too exclusively to the West. But this was hardly a fair judgment. The threat from the West was a real threat, as the fate of Genoa showed. And besides, in the first year of Foscari's reign there had been a great success in the East. In that year the Greek governor of Salonika, the emporium of Thessalian grain (Venice lived on imported grain) and the nothern watchtower of the Aegean, gave or sold his city to Venice rather than lose it to the Turks. So the East, it seemed, was safe. Meanwhile, the republic had obtained an invaluable ally for war in the West. It happened that at this time the greatest condottiere in Italy, the man who had himself recreated the power of the Visconti in Milan, now, on some slight, deserted his master and offered his services to Venice. This was Francesco Bussone, known as Carmagnola. The Venetians could hardly resist such an opportunity. It was against a background of this double security provided by Salonika in the East and Carmagnola in the West that the republic, in 1425, made a league with Florence and declared war on the revived, aggressive power of the Visconti.

Thus, within three years of his accession, Foscari was carrying out the policy that had always been associated with him. There can be no doubt that it was his policy: there exists the speech with which he persuaded the republic to make war. Of course, given the Venetian constitution, one can be sure it was not his policy alone, for he had only influence, not authority. Nevertheless, it seems that it was his influence, combined with circumstances, which weighted and held the scales. Even twelve years later, in 1437, that personal prestige was extraordinarily powerful. In that year the Doge sat, day after day, at the bedside of his son Domenico, who was dying of the plague. Foscari's supporters feared that he, too, would catch the infection, and then what would they do? The lives of many, they said, depended on his: if he were to fail, the fortune and the forward policy of the state would be in peril. Clearly, if men could say this, the Doge was no mere chairman. The forward policy of the state depended particularly on him in 1437, when those initial advantages which had made the western war popular a dozen years earlier had disappeared.

In fact neither Salonika nor Carmagnola lived up to their promise. Salonika was the first to go. In 1430 the Turks captured and sacked it; the slaughter was terrible, the loss final. From now on the Aegean Sea lay open to the Turks, with the wealth of Venice in it, scattered among subject islands whose Greek inhabitants preferred (or thought they preferred) Turkish conquest to Venetian exploitation. In the same year an attempt was made to assassinate the Doge. And as for Carmagnola, like so many condottieri, he proved thoroughly unsatisfactory. At the head of one of the greatest armies that had been seen in Italy, he somehow failed to be as victorious in Venetian as he had been in Milanese service, and he remained suspiciously familiar with his former employer and present enemy, the Duke of Milan. The Venetians offered to make him lord of Milan if he would only conquer it, but still he consumed time and money in mere parades or took cures at the baths of Abano. Finally the Venetians lost patience. With their usual circumspection, they did nothing rashly or openly, but invited Carmagnola to Venice to meet the Doge and discuss future strategy. He never saw the Doge. Instead, he was whisked from the palace to prison, tortured, tried, and condemned. When his sentence was discussed, the Doge voted for mercy, but was overruled, and Carmagnola was sentenced to death and beheaded. That was in 1432. After that the republic employed other, less dangerous condottieri.

So by 1432 Foscari's policy was faced with difficulties on all fronts. He sensed the obstacles, and next year asked to resign his office. It is said that he asked again in 1442 and again in 1446, and this suggests that he was an impulsive man, impatient of obstruction, easily discouraged by defeat. But the Venetian aristocracy, or perhaps his supporters in it, would not allow him to give up his office. On each occasion they reminded him that, by the constitution, he could not resign except wth the assent of the six councilors and the Greater Council. It was an answer which he was later to remember and to use against his enemies.

Meanwhile the forward policy continued. The war for the *terraferma* went on. It was very long, lasting, with brief interludes, for thirty years. It was also very costly; the first ten years alone cost seven million ducats. It had its dramatic incidents—among them the bringing of Venetian ships over the mountains from the river Adige to Lake Garda; it had its disappointments, too—the most bitter being the gradual slide of the Florentines, out of commercial rivalry, toward the side of Milan. But in the end the war was successful. It carried the westward frontier of the *terraferma* to its furthest and final limit, to incorporate the provinces of Brescia and Bergamo, and the Doge solemnly received them as imperial fiefs. He also obtained Ravenna as a papal fief. And before his death he inspired and signed a new treaty—a league with Florence and Milan, Rome and Naples, which was to preserve the liberty of Italy. It would have been a great triumph had it lasted: all we can say is that at least it outlasted Foscari.

So the pageants and the war went on. But meanwhile what of the third feature of Foscari's reign, the enmity of his rivals? This, too, was very long—long and bitter, as Venetian enmities always were. For if Venice, with its exaltation of state service, was free from the strife of parties which ruined every other Italian republic, it was enlivened, even more than the others, by fierce personal and family feuds. In particular, the Doge Foscari never escaped the bitter hatred of the Loredan family. He had defeated them in 1423. They remembered their defeat, and in after years, with their allies the Donà and the Barbarigo, mercilessly persecuted him at his weakest point—his family.

At the time of his election, one objection to Foscari had been his large family, whose members, it was suggested, would feed on the resources of the state. This danger did not materialize, for of his five sons, four died young of the plague. The last survivor, who alone had heirs, and to whom the Doge was devoted, was Jacopo, a young man of cultivated tastes—a Greek scholar and collector of manuscripts—but indiscreet ways. In 1441 his marriage to Lucrezia Contarini had been one of the most magnificent of the many spectacles which the Doge gave to the city. There had been boat races, feasts, and illuminations, with the city adorned in scarlet and cloth of gold, a great tournament before thirty thousand people in the Piazza San Marco, and two hundred and fifty horsemen had ridden in cavalcade over the Grand Canal on a specially built bridge of barges. But in 1445 Jacopo Foscari was secretly denounced for receiving gifts from Filippo Maria Visconti, the Duke of Milan. At that time Francesco Loredan, the nephew of the defeated candidate, was one of the three chiefs of the Council of Ten, the secret political police of the republic. His ally Ermolao Donà was another, and the Ten decided to act at once. They ordered the arrest of Jacopo and excluded the Doge and his kinsmen from all their deliberations on the matter. Then sentence was pronounced: Jacopo was exiled to Nauplia in Greece, and all his goods were confiscated. In vain the Dogaressa begged to see her son; the orders were given, and the name of the Doge himself was placed, with ruthless, impersonal irony, at their head. Before they could be executed there was a hitch, and then, on grounds of health, the place of exile was changed to Treviso, which was both nearer and more comfortable; but the humiliation to the Doge was no less. It was after this bitter defeat that Foscari made his third attempt to resign; but he was forced to remain in office and drink the dregs of the cup.

Before long, however, the Doge was able to score a point. In 1447 he made a moving appeal to the Ten, and the Ten consented, not on grounds of humanity but (a typically Venetian reason) "because it is necessary at this time to have a prince whose mind is free and serene, able to serve the republic," to remit the exile of Jacopo, now sick in body and mind. But the reunion of the Jacob and the Benjamin of the house of Foscari did not last long.

In 1450 the Loredan family found another pretext, and resumed their attack.

That year one of Jacopo Foscari's judges, Ermolao Donà, was murdered, and Jacopo was at once suspected. Again the Doge's son was arrested; he was even tortured; and although nothing was proved and he was probably innocent (it is said that another man afterward confessed to the crime), the Ten, having gone so far, were afraid to go back. They sentenced him, without proof, to exile, and this time there were no second thoughts; he was carried off to Crete. Even in Crete his movements were watched, his indiscretions observed; and in 1456 it was reported to the Ten that he was planning, or at least discussing, revenge with foreign help. The Ten (of whom Jacopo Loredan was now one of the chiefs) immediately decided that the matter was "of the greatest importance"; and once again the Doge's son was fetched back for a trial.

Now began the final tragedy of the Doge's reign, the tragedy which Byron converted into his drama *The Two Foscari*. Before this third trial it was admitted that Jacopo's projects were entirely academic, and that being in Crete, he could do little or nothing to harm the republic; but that made no difference. He was tortured and judged guilty, and the remorseless Jacopo Loredan urged that he be publicly beheaded as a traitor between the columns of the Piazza. Even the Ten drew the line at this, and the prisoner was sentenced to renewed exile in Crete, this time in prison. Before returning to Crete, he was allowed to see his father, now eighty-four years old. He begged the Doge to intercede for him. "Jacopo," replied the old man, "go and obey your country's commands, and seek no more." But when his son had gone, he threw himself upon a chair, weeping and crying, *"O pietà grande!"* Within a few months he was shattered by the news that his last son was dead in Crete.

The Doge's distress was his enemies' opportunity, and they now decided to complete their victory. The Doge, they said, was too old; he was distracted by grief—the grief they had caused him;

he could no longer attend to business. Therefore he must go. The
Council of Ten met and decided to demand his abdication (*see*
opposite). Their message was brought to the Doge by Jacopo
Loredan. But now the old man had his revenge. He turned on
them the argument they had used against him in the past: by the
law, he said, he could not abdicate unless the councilors proposed
and the Greater Council agreed. Here, too, he obeyed his country's laws. Baffled, the Ten consulted again, reinterpreted the law
to suit their convenience, and told the Doge of their reinterpreta-
tion; but still he kept to the old interpretation and would not move.
Finally they sent him an order: he was to resign and clear out of
the ducal palace within eight days. If he did so, he would receive
an adequate salary and a doge's burial; if not, he would be driven
out and all his goods confiscated.

It was a completely illegal demand, but the Doge was power-
less. He gave in. The ducal ring was taken from his finger and
broken, the ducal cap from his head. He promised to leave the
palace. Then, seeing pity in the eye of one of his visitors, he
called to him and, taking his hand, said, "Whose son are you?"
"I am the son of Messer Marin Memmo," was the reply. The Doge
said, "He is my old friend. Ask him to come and visit me so that
we may go in a boat for solace; we will visit the monasteries."
The next day he left the palace. Wearing his old scarlet robe of
state, he stepped forth, bent but unaided except by his staff. As he
went to the stone steps leading down to the water his brother
Marco urged him to go to his gondola by the covered stair. "No,"
replied the Doge, "I will go down by the same stair by which I
came up to my dukedom." A week later he died—of rage, it was
said, on hearing the bells announcing the election of his successor.

The people of Venice were indignant at the indecent deposition
of the Doge who had reigned so long, who had enjoyed all the
honors and prestige of government, whose figure and personality
were so striking, whom the emperors of East and West had visited,
and who had given them such splendid shows. There was much
murmuring against the usurpation of the Ten, and even the Doge's
enemies were now a little ashamed that they had not waited

A RESOLUTION CALLING FOR THE DOGE'S ABDICATION, VOTED BY THE COUNCIL OF TEN, THE PRIVY COUNCIL, AND THE GIUNTA, A BODY OF TWENTY-FIVE NOBLEMEN.

There is no one who does not thoroughly comprehend how useful and altogether how essential to our State and to our affairs is the presence of a Prince, without which, as becomes manifest from the results, the greatest inconvenience and detriment are apt to arise to our State which, since it has by the infinite clemency of our Creator been bequeathed to us by our forefathers hereditary and fair to look upon, we are bound to preserve with all our power and to hold dearer to us than our very life. And although this our city is furnished with holy laws and ordinances, it is of little avail if they be not executed, if the observance of the same be relaxed. The presence of the Prince besides in the councils, at audiences, in the transaction of affairs of state—how desirable it is, how glorious it is, it would be superfluous to point out. All are aware that our most illustrious Prince has vacated his dignity for a great length of time; and from his advanced age it is not at all to be expected that he will be able to return to the exercise of the functions appertaining thereto. How pernicious his absence and incompetence are is more easily understood than explained. Wherefore: it is proposed that by the authority of this most excellent Council and the Giunta the resolution be agreed to that the Privy councilors and the chiefs of the council shall repair to the presence of the most illustrious Prince and declare to him our opinion "that the government of our city and State (which as his Highness knows very well is excessively arduous) cannot be carried on without the constant presence and cooperation of a Prince: also considering how long his Excellency has for personal reasons renounced all share in this government, and that there is no hope that he will be able at any time hereafter to discharge his duties according to the exigencies of this state; and [considering] that his absence is threatening to involve consequences such as we are assured from his affectionate patriotism, he can never desire to witness;—on these grounds which his Excellency in his supreme wisdom will readily appreciate, we with the aforesaid council of Ten and the Giunta have decided upon exhorting and requesting his Serenity, for the evident and necessary welfare of our State—his native land—freely and spontaneously to abdicate, which on many accounts he ought to do as a good Prince and a true father of his country, and especially as we provide that he shall have for his support and proper maintenance from our Office of Salt 1,500 gold ducats a year for life as well as the residue of his salary due to the present day. Also that if it happen that the same most illustrious Prince on this declaration being made known to him shall demand time to consider, he may be told that we are content to wait for such answer till tomorrow at the hour of tierce."

another week for a natural death. When Foscari was dead they gave him a splendid funeral, in spite of the protests of the former Dogaressa at this solemn humbug. He was buried in the church of the Frari, and a majestic Gothic-Rennaissance monument commemorated his achievement—the conquest of the *terraferma*. Meanwhile the Ten withdrew from the invidious limelight, until the furor over their indecent treatment of the old Doge had abated somewhat. But there was no denying that they had won a notable victory. From now on the constitution was not only clearly oligarchical; it was also clear where the center of oligarchical power lay. It lay with that inner ring of self-elected councilors who could mobilize, even against the Doge, the Council of Ten.

Thus ended the long reign of Francesco Foscari. It ended, as it had begun, in bitter personal controversy, and even today historians dispute its significance. It has been said that it was Foscari who diverted the attention of Venice from East to West, sacrificing Salonika and Constantinople to Bergamo and Brescia. This diversion, it is added, led to disastrous consequences fifty years later, when the powers of Europe united against "the insatiable cupidity of the Venetians and their lust for power." And yet, one may answer, could any other doge really have acted differently? Before Foscari's time the dilemma had been there: if the land powers of Europe would not unite against the Turks, a sea power could not defeat them alone; and could Venice ignore the western threat, or the ominous example of Genoa? Other historians have dwelt on the fear of princely despotism; they have represented the Loredan as incorruptible republicans, Catos inexorable in the cause of the constitution. But is there in fact any evidence that Foscari ever entertained thoughts of altering the constitution? Perhaps in his early years he did (though we can only judge from the suspicion he inspired); but how seriously could an old man of eighty have threatened the established power of the oligarchy? In the end it was not he but his enemies who broke the constitution. He submitted to its most humiliating rules, malevolently applied; his foes broke through its last restraints in order to humble him.

Nevertheless it must be admitted that Foscari's reign was crucial in Venetian history. Whatever his personal aims, they were in the end subordinated and absorbed by the impersonal Venetian system. During his term in office the last Milanese republic was converted into the domain of the Medici, but the jealous republicans of Venice, whatever their motives, and whether they were right or wrong in their personal suspicions, positively strengthened their republic. They accepted the policy, and then crushed the personality, of the one man who might conceivably have recreated the old ducal power, so long undermined. And their victory over him was final. After 1457 the republic no longer feared the Doge. Before that date seven doges had been assassinated, nine had been blinded and exiled, twelve had abdicated, one had been sentenced to death and beheaded, two had been deposed. But after that date all is peace inside the republic. The Venetian constitution survived intact through the era of the native princes. It kept its independence when the other Italian states fell under foreign rule; it resisted the Papacy during the Counter Reformation; and it was to be praised, in the seventeenth century, as the most perfect model of government for any mercantile state which aspired to be free, effective, and independent.

VIII.

Federigo da Montefeltro

by DENIS MACK SMITH

For a brief fifty years, a little hill town in the northern Marches was one of the great cultural centers of Europe. Urbino was the birthplace of Raphael and Bramante. Sculptors were drawn there from Milan and Florence, architects from Siena and Dalmatia, painters from Spain and tapestry workers from Flanders. Paolo Uccello worked inside its hospitable walls; so did Piero della Francesca and Melozzo da Forlì. Baldassare Castiglione emigrated from Mantua in order to live there, and was sent as the special envoy of Urbino to England, taking with him a painting commissioned from Raphael as a present for the English King. And as a result of Castiglione's much-translated *Book of the Courtier,* people all over the Western world heard of this remote mountain town, and learned from the standard of Urbino a code of manners, a way of courtesy and refinement, which became the norm of polite behavior.

The duchy of Urbino and its standards of taste in art and manners were created by Federigo da Montefeltro, whose unforgettable broken-nosed profile portrait by Piero della Francesca has helped to make him one of the best known of Renaissance personalities. Earlier Montefeltro princes had won no special reputation either in politics or culture. For three centuries they had governed no more than a few dozen square miles in the Apennines, sometimes as feudatories of the Holy Roman Emperor, but usually owing nominal allegiance to the Pope. The soil and climate were indifferent, but the precipitous hill villages were easily defensible, and their hardy mountaineers fought well, with the result that the rulers of Urbino remained independent, even though they never owned a port on the Adriatic and never penetrated far down the alluvial valleys into the fertile coastal plain of Ancona. Federigo, who ruled from 1444 to 1482, was the greatest of the Montefeltro dynasty. He consolidated several mountain fiefs and extended them into a state three times larger than his original inheritance. His duchy, which reached from the environs of San Marino in the north to beyond Gubbio in the south, was about sixty miles each way at its longest and broadest, and included perhaps four hundred villages and 150,000 inhabitants. Its independence was maintained by playing off one potential enemy against another—Rome against Venice or Florence against Rome—and luckily two of the strongest Italian states, Naples and Milan, were sufficiently remote from Urbino and sufficiently threatened by Rome or Venice to be generally friendly.

Like many prominent contemporaries, Federigo was born illegitimate. As a boy he spent a year as a hostage in Venice and then went to Mantua, where he was taught by Vittorino da Feltre, the greatest educator of Renaissance Italy. Vittorino ran a boarding school where princes mixed with poor scholars and were given a severe classical education based on Latin and mathematics. The aim was to form character as well as mind and body. Federigo was taught frugal living, self-discipline, and a high sense of social obligation. He was made a connoisseur of literature and the arts, and also had to practice the manly sports, riding, dancing, and swordsmanship—all the accomplishments, in fact, which Castiglione later prescribed for the perfect courtier. Religion and scholarship were equally cultivated, but with a practical application: philosophy was made a guide to the art of living, and gracefulness and self-possession were inculcated as training for public life.

As Federigo himself said later, Vittorino had instructed him "in all human excellence."

Few details are known about Federigo's early life. In 1432, at the age of ten, he was knighted by the Emperor, and five years later, after returning from Mantua to Urbino, he was married, after an engagement which dated from his early childhood. A few months later he set out for Lombardy with a company of eight hundred men to learn the art of war under a professional condottiere who was fighting against Gattamelata. Fighting was the occupation to which most contemporary princes were dedicated, and especially so in Urbino, where the Montefeltro family compensated for the poverty of the land and their remoteness from any significant trade routes by selling their services and their army to one side or other in most Italian wars. This was to be Federigo's chosen career. While his half brother Oddantonio succeeded their father as ruler of Urbino in 1443, Federigo himself seemed doomed to the traditionally subordinate life of the poor, illegitimate relation. But in 1444 the young Oddantonio, because of violent indignation against his debaucheries, was assassinated and his body torn to bits by the town mob. At first Federigo seems to have been refused entry to Urbino, but eventually he was chosen to succeed "by the voice of the people" after promising not to revenge the murder.

Probably the chronicler who called this an election by popular acclaim was not romancing, for contemporaries unanimously praised the young Federigo, and later generations looked back to his reign as a golden age. Any patron as generous as he could no doubt buy adulation from that narrow but important group of writers which handed down what was likely to become the verdict of history, but with Federigo there were no dissentient voices even among commentators who did not benefit from his generosity. Unlike many Renaissance rulers, he avoided the accusation of cruelty and extravagant self-indulgence. He was magnanimous to his foes, and was rewarded handsomely when they preferred to surrender to him rather than run the risk of sack. He was also exceptional for his time in never deserting his allies for gain, and never was he known to break his word, not even when urged to do so by a papal legate. This honesty and trustworthiness were unusual in such a treacherous and brutal age. Federigo's great enemy, Sigismondo Malatesta, was in this respect more typical. Sigismondo was no less picturesque, no less refined and tasteful a patron, and equally fierce a fighter, but his atrocious cruelties were legendary; his dishonorable treatment of allies and his brutality toward subjects were common knowledge, and so was his failure to withstand such a prince as Federigo, who possessed the trust of ordinary people.

The biographers of Federigo (Raphael's father was the first of them) were concerned mainly with military exploits, and consequently there is little information about other aspects of his reign. We know, however, that he had to grant a charter of liberties at his accession. Taxes were to be reduced, some kind of public educational and medical service was promised, and the populace was to have some say in electing magistrates. Probably we should have heard further about this charter if he had governed harshly. According to one chronicler, "revisers" were sent round the country to investigate grievances and relieve poverty, and grain from Apulia was stored away so that prices could be kept steady when the harvest failed. Certainly Federigo was more generally accessible than most Renaissance rulers. Vespasiano da Bisticci described how at mealtimes the doors would be opened so that anyone might address him between courses. Furthermore, "When he rode out he met none who did not salute him and ask how he did. He went about with few attendants; none of them armed . . . He would often go afoot through his lands, entering now one shop and now another, and asking the workmen what their calling was, and whether they were in need of aught. So kind was he, that they all loved him as children love their parents. The country he ruled was a wondrous sight." This affability and accessibility were remarkable at a time when assassination was a common form of political behavior. The benevolence of Federigo's despotism was famous throughout Italy. Where his brother was said to have burnt a page alive for some minor lapse, Federigo was merciful to all offenses save blasphemy. The few recorded instances indicate a man who was just and humane, who prudently considered the welfare of his subjects. A ruler who was so often away on campaign could not afford serious discontent at home.

An important reason for this unusual domestic tranquillity was the profits of successful war, which kept taxes low. Federigo's salary, together with the wages of his army, and perhaps not least the booty they captured, were the means by which a poor country for a while became rich, civilized, and content. His employers included two kings of Naples, two dukes of Milan, and three popes, and even in winter, when not fighting, he insisted on a substantial retainer fee from them. He commanded a good price particularly because of his tried loyalty, for Federigo never kept up relations with both sides simultaneously and never surrendered an allegiance until the end of his stipulated *condotta*. His income also reflected the fact that for many years no other general possessed quite his prestige. Less brilliant than many previous condottieri, he was nevertheless more successful than any in avoiding defeat, and both Castiglione and Vespasiano proudly, if not quite accurately, boasted that he lost not a single battle even when heavily out-numbered.

Federigo was known for keeping exceptionally good discipline among troops. When he met the enemy, his usual technique was to be prudent in the early stages of a battle and impetuous and daring the moment he observed some weakness in his foe's deployment. As a young man he had lost an eye in a tournament, but otherwise he was fit and tough. People admired his swift unexpectedness, the mastery and modernity of his complicated siege works, his skill in carrying heavy guns through difficult mountain country, and his tested ability to endure fatigue, hunger, and wounds. Others admired his charity and the pains he took "to mitigate the horrors and miseries of war." Machiavelli derided the safety-first tactics of professional condottieri, and incorrectly asserted that not a single man was killed when Federigo fought the great Colleoni at Molinella in 1467. The two captains certainly met after this battle to exchange civilities, for chivalry was not extinct, but Machiavelli wrongly assumed that wars were necessarily going to be more decisive and more justifiable in the sixteenth century, when they became less humane and more destructive. Federigo had to satisfy his employers, or he would have been without a job. Wars of independence and imperialism were as real in the fifteenth century as later, even if they were smaller and less lethal.

Federigo's first regular patron was the powerful Sforza family, for whom in 1445 he helped to win Pesaro at the same time that Fossombrone was acquired for Urbino. This earned him an excommunication because it was at odds with papal ambitions, and it also increased the enmity of the Malatesta. Sigismondo Malatesta controlled a large stretch of coast above Ancona. His state and Federigo's were too close to avoid friction, and they shared an insecurity and lack of natural frontiers which led to quarrelsomeness and aggression. In between his struggles with Sigismondo, Federigo in 1448 raised an army for the Florentines. Several years later he contracted to serve the Aragonese dynasty in Naples, and this arrangement lasted almost all his life. The throne of Naples was at this point contested by the French Angevins, who found considerable support among the Neapolitan baronage, but Federigo in 1460 helped the Aragonese to resist the invaders, and in the following year he captured the important town of Aquila.

While Federigo was preoccupied in southern Italy, a Malatesta army invaded Urbino and papal territory. The ferocious Sigismondo was therefore "canonized to hell" by the Pope and burnt in effigy before St. Peter's, while his excommunication for heresy, uxoricide, incest, and other crimes was pronounced by Cardinal Nicholas of Cusa. Federigo, as captain general of the Church's forces, seized this opportunity to destroy his rival's power for good. Sigismondo's heir was taken prisoner when Fano fell after a difficult and damaging siege, but Federigo released him without ransom despite the fact that contemporary practice made such hostages a legitimate and profitable asset. In addition to Fano, Senigallia was captured, and all that remained to the Malatesta was Rimini. Sigismondo, on his knees, publicly recanted his atheistical beliefs. Most of the Malatesta empire was claimed by the Pope and the papal nephews. Federigo, however, was allowed some fifty townships, which made him more powerful than any other ruler throughout the Marches and the Romagna. Although still a pigmy among the giant states of Milan, Venice, and Naples, he sometimes held the balance of power in Italy.

At this time the Papacy was trying to enforce its suzerainty and taxation rights over the seignorial families who ruled in central Italy. Pius II had exploited the rivalry between Montefeltro and Malatesta, employing one to subdue the other, and in 1465 his successor, Paul II, appointed Federigo *gonfaloniere*, or captain, of the Church's forces, in order to extend papal power still further. The condottiere from Urbino was now a famous man in Italy. In 1467 he was made commander of a league of states alarmed at the aggressive imperialism of Venice. The Venetians, retreating before the Turks on the far shore of the Adriatic, were attempting to compensate for these losses by pushing their empire westward and southward in Italy, to the consternation of their neighbors and the Pope. Federigo's own state was among those upon which both Rome and Venice might have ambitions, and this dual threat increased in direct proportion to his general political success.

In 1468 Sigismondo Malatesta died, and the Pope tried to annex Rimini. At this point Federigo, who had hitherto been more frightened of Venice, recognized the danger of further papal aggrandizement. He was a devout and loyal son of the Church, but not without qualification, for he could see that Venice and Rome between them were gradually swallowing up the Romagna. Even more alarming, the popes were trying to conquer principalities for their sons and nephews before another family succeeded them in their sacred office. Against this danger Montefeltro and Malatesta made common cause out of self-preservation, and instead of renewing his lapsed *condotta* with the Pope, Federigo supported the claims of Roberto Malatesta to Rimini. The ruler of Urbino, as captain of a league which included Naples and Milan, as well as other Romagnol *signori,* routed the papal army at Mulazzano.

Federigo's first wife, Gentile Brancaleoni, had died in 1457 leaving no children. He then married Battista, daughter of Alessandro Sforza of Pesaro. Battista's face is almost as well known to us from Piero's portrait as her husband's. Married at thirteen, she died at twenty-five, leaving one son, many daughters, and the reputation of being a formidable bluestocking who had governed the state in her husband's absence and could extemporize publicly in Latin. Federigo's half-sisters had married into the neighboring dynasties of Sforza, Gonzaga, and Malatesta; two of his daughters were bestowed upon papal families, the Colonna and della Rovere, and a third upon Roberto Malatesta, the illegitimate son of his old enemy. The circle of appropriate families being limited, there was an inevitable tendency to inbreed.

In 1472, the year Battista died, Federigo was asked by Lorenzo de' Medici to raise an army against Volterra in Tuscany. (Lorenzo was defending the mining interests of Florentine citizens against nationalization in Volterra.) The military task was easy, but after the town had surrendered, Federigo could not restrain his soldiers from a terrible sack. Discipline in mercenary armies was always a problem, especially since the prospect of loot was an inducement for enlisting recruits, but this was a solitary lapse on Federigo's part. For himself he seized only a polyglot Bible of great rarity and beauty, and he was then escorted in triumph to a civic banquet in Florence and given a helmet adorned by Pollaiuolo. Another distinction received soon afterward was the Order of the Garter from England, and this emblem became a common motif in the decoration of his palace. Such was his reputation outside Italy that special embassies arrived not only from England and Hungary but from Persia and Trebizond. A further triumph came in 1474, when Sixtus IV, solemnly received him in St. Peter's, changed his traditional title of Count to Duke. This acknowledged that Urbino had now reached a special position of independence and strength that distinguished it from other small city-states. It also acknowledged the Pope's need for military support for his nephews, and the formal concession of the title was designed to seal the alliance.

Federigo served Sixtus well. He tamed the insubordinate ruler of Città di Castello in Umbria, and in 1479 he campaigned against Florence after the Pope had tried and failed to assassinate Lorenzo de' Medici. Papal ambitions, however, soon became dangerous again when Sixtus began planning a conquest of Ferrara for yet another nephew. Federigo wrote to the Pope, urging him to turn against the Moslems who had just won a foothold in southern Italy; but the head of Christendom was more anxious to establish his family than to oppose the Turkish advance. As a result, war broke out over Ferrara, and Federigo aligned himself against papal aggression with Naples, Florence, Milan, Mantua, and Bologna, while his son-in-law, Roberto Malatesta, led the opposing papal forces. In the malarial swamps of Ferrara the rival commanders were stricken with the fever which was the greatest scourge of Renaissance Italy, and Federigo and Roberto died on the same day, September 10, 1482.

For a time Federigo's son and successor, Guidobaldo, was able to maintain the model state of Urbino, continuing his father's lavish patronage of the arts until his lack of success as a general lessened the profits of warfare upon which the economy depended. Then, in 1502, Pope Alexander VI persuaded Guidobaldo to loan the papal army his artillery, and at this crucial moment the Pope's son, Cesare Borgia, swept down on Urbino, forced its ruler to flee, and appropriated the priceless art collection, much of which he sold to pay his troops.

Perhaps Federigo himself would have fared no better. He had been the last of the great condottieri, and lived at a time when defense was much easier than attack. Shortly after his death that day had passed; heavy artillery became more common and more efficient; and when it did the fortified hill towns and castles were suddenly vulnerable. The superiority of new weapons spelled ruin for the small Renaissance princedoms. A decade after his death, the perennial conflicts between Italian cities and families led to an invasion of the peninsula by France and Spain, and it was these new, large nation-states which were to dominate the next period of European history. For three centuries Italy was a convenient location where foreign armies could fight each other; and whereas

Federigo had taken care to conduct his wars abroad, Urbino itself now became a battleground. By 1530 a series of invasions and counter-invasions had sacked Rome and Florence and desolated that world of small city-states which had engendered the Renaissance. Much of the surplus wealth which enlightened princes had once used for endowing culture and the arts was dissipated, and in this strange new world Urbino was too small and too awkwardly situated between rival empires to survive.

Federigo da Montefeltro is not remembered for his battles; he made no notable contribution to the art of war; his dynasty and dukedom disappeared. The one thing which survived intact was the memory of Federigo and his court of humanists and artists. In retrospect he and his son were spoken of alongside the magnificent Lorenzo. They were children of their time in a love of lavish display, in their burning drive for self-expression and a competitive urge for prestige. These instincts without doubt contributed in part to their devotion to art and learning, though both of them showed well enough that they also possessed a disinterested love of all things beautiful. Certainly they were far above all other contemporary rulers in character and intellectual refinement. Through them Urbino became a celebrated center of culture which attracted men of talent and renown from all of Europe; it was the place to which the Doria, Orsini, and Farnese families, as well as wealthy parents in other countries, sent their children to be educated. Castiglione, nostalgically recollecting that Federigo, in his day, was "the light of Italy," described life at Urbino in his delightful book, *The Courtier,* in which he recorded a portrait of the model gentleman. As Vittoria Colonna wrote to him, "I do not wonder that you have depicted the perfect courtier, for you had only to hold a mirror before you, and set down what you saw there." The conversations recorded in *The Courtier* took place in the palace which Federigo had built at Urbino.

Books of all kinds were Federigo's greatest joy, and Vespasiano described his efforts to build the great library in Urbino: "We come now to consider in what high esteem the Duke held all Greek and Latin writers, sacred as well as secular. He alone had a mind to do what no one had done for a thousand years or more; that is, to create the finest library since ancient times. He spared neither cost nor labor, and when he knew of a fine book, whether in Italy or not, he would send for it. It is now fourteen or more years since he began the library, and he always employed, in Urbino, in Florence, and in other places, thirty or forty scribes in his service . . . There are numerous Greek books by various authors, which when he was not able to get them otherwise, he sent for them, desiring that nothing should be wanting in any tongue which it was possible to acquire. There were to be seen Hebrew books, all that could be found in that language, beginning with the Bible, and all those who have commented upon it, Rabbi Moses and other commentators. Not only are those Hebrew books the Holy Scriptures, but also on medicine, on philosophy, and in all branches, all that could be acquired in that tongue.

"His lordship having completed this worthy task at the great expense of more than thirty thousand ducats, among the other excellent and praiseworthy arrangements which he made was this, that he undertook to give to each writer a title, and this he desired should be covered with crimson embellished with silver. He began, as has been noted above, with the Bible, as the foremost of all, and had it covered, as was said, with gold brocade. Then beginning with all the Doctors of the Church, he had each one covered with crimson and embellished with silver, and so with the Greek Doctors as with the Latins. As well philosophy, history, and books on medicine, and all the modern Doctors; in such a manner that there are innumerable volumes of this kind, a thing gorgeous to behold.

"In this library all the books are beautiful in the highest degree, all written with the pen, not one printed, that it might not be disgraced thereby; all elegently illuminated, and there is not one that is not written on kidskin. There is a singular thing about this library, which is not true of any other; and this is, that of all the writers, sacred as well as profane, original works as well as translations, not a single page is wanting from their works in so far as they are in themselves complete; which can not be said of any other library, all of which have portions of the works of a writer, but not all; and it is a great distinction to possess such perfection."

Vespasiano had helped to collect this library. "Some time before," he wrote, "I went to Ferrara, being at Urbino at his lordship's court, and having catalogues of all the libraries of Italy, commencing with that of the Pope, of St. Mark's at Florence, of Pavia—and I had even sent to England to obtain a catalogue of the library of the university of Oxford—I compared these with that of the Duke, and I saw that all were faulty in one particular; that they had numerous copies of the same work, but they had not all the works of one writer complete as this had; nor were there writers of every branch as in this." Virtually the whole corpus of known classics was in the library, as well as Avicenna, Averroes, and medieval texts. Federigo was also a patron of contemporary literature. Ficino, Landino, Poggio, and Piero della Francesca dedicated writings to this man whom the humanist Piatti eulogized as *oraculum totius Italiae.*

The Duke was a competent Latinist in an age when close attention to the example of olden times was recommended for statesmen and generals. He was also an early enthusiast of Greek and hired instructors to teach it. He was able to discuss the Trojan war with Pius II and dared to contradict that learned scholar about the geography of Asia Minor. He liked to have Livy's histories read aloud at mealtimes, and was especially fond of Tacitus and the *Commentaries* of Caesar. "To return to letters," Vespasiano wrote, "the Duke of Urbino was well versed therein, not only in history and in the Holy Scriptures, but also in philosophy, which he studied many years under a distinguished teacher, Maestro Lazzaro, afterwards for his merits made Bishop of Urbino. He was instructed by Maestro Lazzaro in the *Ethics* of Aristotle, with and without comments, and he would also dispute over the difficult passages. He began to study logic with the keenest understanding, and he argued with the most nimble wit that was ever seen. After he had heard the *Ethics* many times, comprehending them so thoroughly that his teachers found him hard to

cope with in disputation, he studied the *Politics* assiduously . . .
Indeed, it may be said of him that he was the first of the *Signori*
who took up philosophy and had knowledge of the same. He was
ever careful to keep intellect and virtue to the front, and to learn
some new thing every day."

With all this, the Duke was devoutly religious. He heard Mass
daily, and delighted in discussing religion with the abbot or mother
superior of the monastic houses which he had endowed. He not
only knew the Scriptures well, but was familiar with the great
Doctors of the early Church and possessed an extensive theo-
logical library. He developed "a strong predilection" for the works
of Saint Thomas Aquinas. He was no puritan, yet despite his four
illegitimate children he was a moral man and, as befitted a pupil
of Vittorino, recognized no dichotomy between humanist and
Christian ideals.

Federigo's taste and qualities of mind were embodied most
obviously in his famous palace at Urbino, for to him architecture
was not only queen of the arts but the very summit of intellectual
as well as aesthetic activity. Beginning around 1450 and building
slowly, Federigo gradually amplified his ideas, and in 1468, after
searching and failing to find an architect in the Tuscany which he
so admired, he chose Luciano Laurana as chief architect. After
Laurana there arrived Francesco di Giorgio, the foremost engineer in Italy, who dedicated to the Duke a celebrated treatise on
architecture and gratefully acknowledged an indebtedness to his
employer for many technical hints about fortification. Five architects and engineers are mentioned in a surviving list of palace
officers.

The same list reveals the royal scale of life in the great palace.
There were five hundred people in the court: in addition to knights
and men-at-arms, these included two hundred servants, four teachers, an astrologer, five "readers aloud at meals," four men who
transcribed manuscripts, two organists, the keeper of the blood-
hounds, and a man who tended the camel-leopard.

But it was the buildings which struck people most. Lorenzo de'
Medici admired them, and they were to astonish Montaigne and

a long succession of travelers. Federigo had furnished his palace,
Castiglione wrote, "so well with every suitable thing that it
seemed not a palace but a city in the form of a palace; and furnished it not only with what is customary such as silver vases,
wall hangings of the richest cloth of gold, silk, and other things,
but for ornament he added countless ancient statues of marble
and bronze, rare paintings, and musical instruments of every sort;
nor did he wish to have anything there that was not most rare and
excellent." Vespasiano da Bisticci was even more enthusiastic.
(As a Florentine, Vespasiano judged by the highest standards.)
"As to architecture it may be said that no one of his age, high or
low, knew it so thoroughly. We may see, in the buildings he constructed, the grand style and the due measurement and proportion,
especially in his palace, which has no superior amongst the buildings of the time, none so well considered, or so full of fine things.
Though he had his architects about him, he always first realized
the design and then explained the proportions and all else; indeed,
to hear him discourse thereanent, it would seem that his chief
talent lay in this art; so well he knew how to expound and carry
out its principles."

Vasari was another Florentine who commented admiringly on
the commodious apartments of Urbino's palace, and its stairways
which were "more convenient and agreeable than any that had
existed previously." Windows and doorways in admirable proportion, a graceful court with slender columns, a hanging garden,
the great library, and room after room with splendid decoration
in stucco and marble relief—all testifying to the sensibility as well
as the munificence of the Duke. Intarsia, marquetry, polychrome
marble, and *trompe-l'oeil* work on the walls represented what was
best in current fashion all over Italy. Ambrogio da Milano and
Domenico Rosselli of Pistoia were employed to design ornamental
motifs on jambs, pediments, and chimney pieces, upon which the
garter of England and the eagle of Montefeltro were frequently
found. Typical of Federigo was that alongside his religious chapel,
and with the same proportions, was another chapel dedicated
to the Muses; and in his study were twenty-eight portraits of

famous men in world history, among whom Homer was alongside Aquinas, Ptolemy with Saint Ambrose, and Seneca with Solomon. Typical also of this Renaissance prince was an inscription round the interior court which told how the great Federigo had raised this palace for his own glory and for his posterity.

In all respects, Federigo had represented the best in his age, and his example endured long after he had passed away. Through his practice the teachings of Vittorino inspired a small but noble society which, even when conquered politically, made a conquest of all Europe. At Urbino could be found an intellectual elite which believed that an integrated and disciplined education would result in proper behavior and a proper sense of duty toward God and man. Federigo's classical upbringing and intellectual curiosity in no way undermined, but rather reinforced the teachings of orthodox religion. Nor did he tend to that all too common form of humanism which despised science; on the contrary, Vespasiano praised the Duke's skill in geometry and arithmetic. As for the arts, Federigo was enthusiastic about more than architecture. His musical tastes perhaps show the influence of contemporary Flanders, the same influence which brought Justus of Ghent and Flemish servants and textile artisans to his court. "He delighted greatly in music," Vespasiano noted, "understanding vocal and instrumental alike, and maintained a fine choir with skilled musicians and many singing boys. He had every sort of instrument in his palace and delighted in their sound, also the most skillful players. He preferred delicate to loud instruments, caring little for trombones and the like."

Anything loud and harsh was anathema at the court of Urbino. Dress had to be sober, demeanor quiet, conversation lively but gentle. Women were given an active and respected place in this world, setting new standards for polite society. Vittorino's educational goal had been to create the complete all-round person who was courteous, upright, sensitive, but at the same time active. Federigo himself was such a man. He possessed a robust physique which resisted wounds and great hardship, yet the rough practice of war left his finer feelings unimpaired. Everyone knew him

to be a man of honor as well as courage. His official portraits
show him not so much as a warrior but as an intellectual, either
reading, contemplating, listening to a lecture, or at prayer. Unlike many Renaissance princes, he lived without excess, "eating
plain food and no sweetmeats," and the five hundred people who
composed his court followed as orderly an existence as in a monastery: "Here was no romping or wrangling, but everyone spoke
with becoming modesty."

What little we know about this court of Urbino gives us a
precious insight into the civilization of the Renaissance in Italy
at its most admirable. Piero della Francesca's work has partially
perished, the superb ducal library was swallowed up by the Vatican,
and Federigo's portraits were scattered to Florence, Milan, and
Windsor. But time cannot easily erase his memory and example.
Had he been more representative of his class, the course of the
Renaissance might have followed a still more brilliant path.

IX.

Beatrice and Isabella d'Este

by MARIA BELLONCI

The stories of the two sisters, Beatrice and Isabella d'Este, are not easily interwoven in a single brief account, nor would either of them have relished such a thing, for they were lively, even peremptory individualists. Then, too, the span of their lives was very different. Of Beatrice, who died when she was twenty-two, we know only the transports, the vehemences, the proud and ambitious passions of adolescence. On the other hand, we know, step by step, Isabella's magistral development from youthful potential to the maturity that unfolds and reveals the meaning of a human life. They were born in Ferrara one year apart, Isabella in 1474 and Beatrice in 1475, thus preceding their four brothers —Alfonso, Ferrante, Ippolito, and Sigismondo.

The Este, one of the most ancient dynasties in Italy, had dominated Ferrara—a strategic area between Lombardy, Venice, and Emilia—and the broad luxuriant valley of the Po since the thirteenth century. They belonged to the Guelph party and for centuries had fought the Ghibellines in defense of the Church— and even fought the Church on those occasions when the popes had sought to meddle unduly in their affairs. These struggles, added to embroilments with neighboring powers or within the

139

Este family, had forged a race of men who, no matter what their individual temperaments, were bold statesmen. In proof of this, the Ferrarese, a people proud to the point of arrogance and brave to the point of temerity (a Ferrarese proverb states that no man is too poor to own a dagger), never, not even when sorely provoked, rebelled against their masters.

It was Niccolò III, coming to power in 1402, who with the unsparing energy of his forebears consolidated the domain on a grand scale. Niccolò III was a resolute soldier, an astute manipulator of circumstance, and a man of constructive intelligence, who founded a university and was so solicitous of the people's welfare as to stipulate in his will that the monies allocated for his own funeral should be donated instead to public charity. Variously magnanimous and cruel (he ordered his son Ugo and his second wife, Parisina, beheaded when he discovered that they were lovers), Niccolò had exceptional sons who reigned in succession after him, the first two illegitimate, the third legitimate. Leonello, a level-headed, shrewd politician, sowed the seeds of the flowering of humanism in Ferrara; Borso, also a statesman of peace, was equally devoted to the arts. The first legitimate son to rule was Ercole, a man whose temperament was so icy that it won him the nicknames "North Wind" and "The Diamond."

In 1473, two years after he ascended the throne at the age of forty, Ercole made the most political of marriages, wedding Leonora of Aragon, the daughter of King Ferrante of Naples, who was at the time a very powerful sovereign. The bride was beautiful—indeed, more than beautiful. Naturally regal, endowed with sound bourgeois sense and queenly courage, she was a sensitive, warm woman in whose company even the chilly nature of her husband was somewhat thawed.

Into this noble house and into a court traditionally cultivated and schooled in all the humanistic sciences, Isabella and Beatrice d'Este were born. From birth their destinies seem both divergent and parallel, patterned in counterpoint. Isabella, the first child, was born in May, 1474. She was welcomed with enthusiasm by parents, court, and populace, who saw in the blonde, softly rounded, comely infant girl the herald of the male, the heir to come. Beatrice was born a year later, in June, 1475, and the arrival of this second girl aroused no joy whatever. For her there were no celebrations, royal or popular, and no sign of love except perhaps the slightly humiliated tenderness of a mother who was beginning to feel marked by the most mortifying attribute of a princess—that of being "the mother of females." Both infants were given the names of queens, Isabella being called after her grandmother, the Queen of Naples, and Beatrice named for her aunt, who was wife to Matthias Corvinus, King of Hungary. One year passed and, fortunately, a son was born; Alfonso was received with noisy jubiliation and festivities by all Ferrara. The next year another son, Ferrante, arrived. The girl infants had been redeemed.

Ferrante was born in September, 1477, in the Neapolitan palace of the grandfather whose name he took. That year the King, who was even less old in feeling than in fact, had married for the second time, taking as wife the delicate, elegant Giovanna of Aragon. Leonora was bid to pay her respects to her father and stepmother, and she went to Naples carrying with her not Alfonso —the heir had to remain in Ferrara—but the two girls and the still unborn child. The King of Naples, a dissipated man, richly endowed with ambiguous charms and a taste for the grandiose, took an immediate fancy to Beatrice. He recognized in her the long face and heavy cheeks, the jet-black hair and eyes, and the sulky, heavy-lidded glance of the true Aragon. His marriage was duly celebrated, and Leonora's second son was born shortly there-after, whereupon she was recalled in haste to Ferrara by Duke Ercole, who sniffed the scent of war in the air. She took only Isabella with her, leaving Beatrice and Ferrante in Naples, where they stayed for eight years. The little Este children played with their cousins, among whom was Isabella of Aragon, betrothed to Gian Galeazzo Sforza, who would one day clash with Beatrice in a mortal match.

In her grandfather's court in Naples, Beatrice learned that pride is vital and splendid, that every gesture of King and nobles was governed by an etiquette compounded equally of pomp and fantasy, and she realized, too, that power must be deserved. Accordingly, she began then to develop the intrepid patience that would stand her in such good stead when she returned to Ferrara to find herself in a position secondary in every respect. There was no doubt about it; the child who reigned in the Este palace was the elder sister, the gay and witty and wise Isabella. Everyone adored Isabella. No one had ever seen such an intense and vivacious feminine intelligence, such a felicitously inventive art in arranging things to her own liking while capturing the consent of others. Even the judicious Leonora was beguiled into calling her "my dearest and sweetest of daughters." Perhaps Isabella was not as beautiful as they say: she was not very tall and her features were not perfect, but she had a clear, rosy-cheeked complexion and a bearing of incomparable elegance. And her intelligence was prodigious. Her teachers were stunned when she translated smoothly and rapidly a selection from Virgil's *Bucolics* or a letter of Cicero; she mastered Greek and Latin grammar, committed Terence and Virgil to memory, learned to perform songs and madrigals on the lute, was first in perfecting the steps of a new dance, embroidered faultlessly, conversed—and held her own—with ambassadors.

The year 1480 was a year of engagements in the Este house, and it brought Isabella the worst bit of sheer bad luck that she was to suffer in her whole life. In April a marriage contract was signed between her and Francesco Gonzaga, heir of the neighboring Marquis of Mantua. Scarcely a month later, an ambassador arrived from Milan to ask for Isabella's hand on behalf of Lodovico Sforza. Il Moro, as he was called, was the guardian of his young nephew, the Duke of Milan, but in actuality Lodovico was master of both his nephew and half of Italy. Since Duke Ercole would never offend the Marquis of Mantua, who was his friend and ally, by reneging on agreements already signed, he took advantage of Il Moro's suit to marry off both of the pawns he held in the game of alliances. Let the first daughter go to the Marquis of Mantua, and let the second, who was the equal of her sister—

legitimate, healthy, intelligent, and cultivated—go to Il Moro. (Alfonso d'Este, his eldest son, was already affianced to Anna Sforza, the Duke of Milan's sister.) Lodovico was not enthusiastic, and he accepted this engagement of expediency with perceptible disappointment.

Happily, a fresh and quite unusual relationship developed between Isabella and Francesco; the innocent and touching charm of the girl surprised and beguiled her fiancé, a vigorous and already experienced fifteen-year-old youth, even before it made him fall in love with her. But between Beatrice and Lodovico there was nothing of this sort. He who was judged the first man in all Italy, and who was certainly one of the richest, scarcely remembered the dark-haired girl, twenty-five years younger than he, who awaited him in Ferrara. On the contrary. Surrounded by the elaborate pomp of his court, he was flaunting his passion for the beautiful, exquisitely mannered Cecilia Gallerani, the unofficial queen of Milan. It is not certain whether Beatrice knew of her rival or not, for contemporary accounts record only the silence of the young Este girl in this period.

In February of 1490, ten years after her engagement, Isabella went as a bride to the castle in Mantua, her resolute, slim sixteen years transported there in the triumphal carriage designed by Ercole de' Roberti; his too, was the hand that painted the thirteen chests that followed her, in which her elegant trousseau was packed. She was followed also by her father, mother, sister, her three brothers, the whole band of her Este relatives, and the acclamations of seventeen thousand spectators. Isabella was going to a youthful court, since her delightful parents-in-law, Federigo and Margherita, who so warmly wanted her in their family, had died while still young. Her husband was twenty-five, his two brothers twenty-one and sixteen. Her new eighteen-year-old sister-in-law was Elisabetta Gonzaga, a woman of pale and heraldic beauty, who was the wife of Guidobaldo, Duke of Urbino. (For a time no one suspected the burning secret of the unconsummated marriage which Elisabetta endured with love and shame and a passional exhaustion which bordered on despair.)

That February, the most gloomy, foggy month in the year for lacustrine Mantua, was for Isabella a period of acquisition, confirmed by a whole series of new possessions beginning with her husband. She served no novitiate as daughter-in-law, but came at once into both title and power, rising to the demands of her role with the sparkling glance and lightness of step that lent wings to her sixteen years. Isabella realized that her marriage had the rigorous political significance of an alliance between reigning families, for on this score she had learned her father's lesson well, and she responded to her husband's passion like a woman who appreciates the quality of being warmly involved in marriage without being swept away or losing her own identity thereby. As for her young husband, one of the most ugly and fascinating men in Italy, he was the brave soldier, the complete gentlemen, a graceful and entertaining conversationalist in the Lombard style, a lover of gentle sensuality—and so delightfully ingenuous as to have his humanists compose poems that he sent to his literary-minded wife as his own. He, too, was overcome with admiration for Isabella, but his admiration, which perforce grew greater day by day, was destined to alter in kind. Francesco Gonzaga scarcely realized it, but presently he began to lose confidence in his wife who was like no one else, and who, while obedient to his smallest wish, seemed always to protect a growing independence of her own. Yet she was so loyal, so adroit in sensing whatever could benefit the little Mantuan state and the Gonzaga family, that it was difficult to find cause for reproach. The new Marchioness of Mantua was clearly the pride of the city; her praises were sung, indeed, throughout Italy.

In Ferrara, Beatrice was awaiting her husband. She should have married immediately after her sister, but Lodovico Il Moro was bound to his Cecilia Gallerani and showed not the least concern about joining his betrothed. However, Ercole d'Este was not a man to accept even a small affront, and at a certain point he allowed a hiss of irritation to reach Lodovico's ear. Il Moro, knowing that he needed Ferrara to protect Lombardy against the threat of its centuries-old enemy, the republic of Venice, and further pressured by the marriage pact between his niece Anna and the Este heir apparent, finally brought himself to a decision. And once he had decided, he threw the gates of the Lombard palaces wide, opened the coffers of his treasury, and set in motion the mighty machinery of the Milanese court, which teemed with artists, poets, mathematicians, scholars, and a spirited nobility well disposed toward any courtly enterprise. The wedding date was set for January, 1491, and the place chosen was the castle in Pavia. Whereupon not a day passed without messengers arriving in Ferrara from Milan; they brought gifts, like the famous necklace of pearls strung with flowerets of gold and embellished with splendid drops of rubies, pearls, and emeralds; the masters of ceremonies came to arrange for the bride's journey—and to recommend that Beatrice bring many embroidered and bejeweled gowns; artists came, like Gian Cristoforo Romano, sculptor and engraver, accomplished lute player, and a man of wide literary attainments, who did the bust of Beatrice that is now preserved in the Louvre.

With an intent, childish frown, Beatrice set about preparing herself for her unknown future, and she scarcely noticed the fearsome and memorable trip, as the ice-encrusted *bucentaurs* passed between the snowy banks of the canals. They arrived, finally, in a Pavia blanketed in snow, but inside the castle everything exuded warmth, wealth, and ease. Lodovico led his bride and her entourage through the princely dwelling, judged the most sumptuous in the world. At the last, he showed them its greatest treasure, the library begun by Gian Galeazzo Visconti and now rich in illuminated volumes and Greek and Latin manuscripts that Sforza had had copied in the most remote sanctuaries where they were preserved. In the face of all this splendor Beatrice appeared reserved, which everyone took to mean that she was timid. She had, in any case, no time to recover her self-possession after the wedding (which took place on January 17, the day chosen by the astrologers as propitious), for the next morning Il Moro left for Milan, to arrange, he said, for the celebrations, on which a legion of artists captained by Leonardo da Vinci and Bramante from Urbino were assigned to work. Yet how could one forget that Cecilia Gallerani was living there in the castle?

Eventually, the whole company moved on to Milan, and the spectacle in the great Lombard city surpassed belief: imaginatively staged tournaments, elegant dances, theatricals, masquerades, concerts of rare music, and fantasies of every kind. Energy, grandeur, verve, intelligence, and beauty joined to compose around the bride —who until yesterday had been quite obscure—a magnificent show of which she was the sole heroine. She could, it seemed, be sure even of her husband, from the moment she realized that her youth attracted him. She led him on to fondle her, used every charm to beguile him into kissing her before everyone; she offered him an olive-toned girlish face that was flushed and alight with happiness; everything she did expressed her joy in having been called to so full a life. Before the eyes of her startled mother and sister, Beatrice let go; this was her moment, and it was as if she cut herself off from all else in a frenetic drive to seize it.

Once back in Mantua, Isabella saw to it that she was kept informed daily of what was going on in Milan. The accounts that reached her told of a whirl of amusements; of a morning, Beatrice, Galeazzo di Sanseverino, and Diodato the jester would set out in a carriage, singing three-part songs. They fished, they lunched, they played ball and fished again, and returned home in the evening deliciously exhausted. Beatrice won quick ascendancy over her husband, and if she did not succeed in dislodging Cecilia Gallerani from the castle, she did manage to break off, officially at least, that lady's relationship with Il Moro. In 1491 Cecilia married Count Bergamini, shortly after she gave birth to a son by Lodovico.

Beatrice never wearied of thinking up masquerades, jokes, or expeditions, with herself and her ladies dressed like commoners and spoiling for a squabble with some plebeians. His wife's exploits were irresistibly amusing to Il Moro, who laughed and applauded the girl. In Milan, Beatrice had found her cousin again—that Isabella of Aragon with whom she had played at the court of Naples some years before. From the day Beatrice arrived, she had had to concede first place in the city to Isabella, acknowledging the unchallengeable primacy of her position as wife of the actual Duke, Gian Galeazzo Sforza. However, Isabella of Aragon's greatness of spirit, her courage, and the exquisite refinement of her nature (later, her court was considered an incomparable school for pages and courtiers) did not suffice in her efforts to support her husband, given his weaknesses. The young Duke of Milan appeared to combine the vices of his Visconti and Sforza forebears, although in him they were enfeebled by a congenital fraility that enervated both his physical and intellectual capacities to the point of decay. The courageous daughter of King Alfonso took an unblinking view of her present and her future. The desire for power that she had recognized in Gian Galeazzo's uncle and guardian was now increased by Beatrice's appetite, which had all the fierceness of youthful passion. And the moment was propitious for the ambitious couple. The French King, Charles VIII, was girding himself for the conquest of the kingdom of Naples; the Borgia Pope, Alexander VI, was unable to dissuade him; and Il Moro favored the foreigners' coming, calculating that in this way he could be quit once and forever of all difficulties with the Aragons, who were the natural protectors of Isabella and her children. Without a thought for her grandfather, King Ferrante, who had so doted on her, Beatrice abetted her husband ardently. When in January, 1493, Beatrice's first son was born—Ercole, later called Massimilliano—and royal celebrations were held in his honor, the unfortunate Duchess Isabella of Aragon wept her eyes out.

But her protests accomplished nothing. Late in 1494, Charles VIII was in Italy, received with a whirlwind of festivities by Lodovico and by Beatrice, who dazzled the King, even if she could not prevent some of his French followers from maliciously evaluating her and her displays of costume and charm with the observation that "the husk is worth more than the kernel." At Pavia the tragic colloquy between Isabella of Aragon and the French King took place, in which Isabella fell to her knees before him, in tears. With a vague promise of protection for the Sforza children, Charles VIII left. While the French King was on his way to the easy conquest of Naples, the ailing Gian Galeazzo succumbed to tuberculosis; the young Duke's last request was to see his horses and his greyhounds.

Lodovico quickly set in motion the plan he had long since prepared, and had himself proclaimed master of Milan by his fellow citizens. Shortly thereafter Emperor Maximilian granted the title to the dukedom to him and to his direct heirs, disregarding Gian Galeazzo's son. The fame and fortune of Beatrice, now crowned Duchess of Milan and applauded and sung and glorified by all, glowed brilliantly above the downfall of Isabella of Aragon.

But the Italian states quickly realized that the French King was not a guest to be taken into the house so casually, and they hastened to repair the damage already done. Even Milan joined the league established among Venice, Mantua, the Pope, and other principalities, for Il Moro had come to see that if foreign invasions were dangerous for all, they were most dangerous for him, since Charles made no secret of his wish to annex the duchy of Milan, which, he said, was his by right of inheritance. The armies gathered, and to avoid being captured in the kingdom he had just conquered, Charles VIII withdrew rapidly up the peninsula, and at Fornovo di Taro met the allied armies of the league in a battle from which he managed, as a result of the Italians' incompetence, to escape and to return to France. Italy rejoiced in her recovered liberty, and in Mantua, Isabella rejoiced to see her husband, Marquis Francesco Gonzaga, captain general of the league, the hero of Italy's liberation.

As the characters of the Este sisters became more differentiated, a disquieting rivalry gradually unfolded; it was in no sense petty, for both were women of noble spirit and bound by family loyalties, but it was perceptible, nevertheless. Beatrice's accent on luxury was too loud, verging on the satanic. Everyone found her eighty-four new dresses, heavily embroidered with gold thread, jewels, and pearls, excessive; they hung in a great room that, as her mother, Leonora, observed with graceful irony, resembled a "sacristy hung with all the canonicals." Too many rooms were too full of silver, ivories, precious glass, paintings, perfumes, lutes, clavichords, in quantities sufficient to "fill all the shops." Her unchecked imperiousness, her inconsiderate way of treating people about her, her cruel little games (she used to terrify ladies in waiting by pretending to set her horses upon them at an unbridled gallop), were in the same measure her way of vindicating her humiliated adolescence. When Isabella realized that the festivities and gifts that always awaited her in Milan were contrived to oppress her with honors, she found excuses to accept no further invitations. The immense wealth and the traditional magnificence of the Sforza court allowed Beatrice to have about her men like Bramante and Leonardo; she made her presence felt even in politics, and could engage in well-informed arguments with heads of state.

Another source of bitterness for Isabella was their relative maternal status. In the Sforza household there were two sons, Ercole and Francesco; in the Gonzaga household there were two daughters, Eleonora and Margherita. When Beatrice sent her congratulations on the birth of Eleonora, there was a hint of self-satisfaction in her including the greetings of her little son to the newborn girl. Isabella was so infuriated that when she bore her second daughter, she insisted that the infant be removed from the sumptuous cradle which had been prepared for a boy. But the fabulous life story of Beatrice hung suspended by the thread of fortune that had created it. Something had already gone wrong when, around 1495, Il Moro had fallen in love with an exquisite lady of the court, Lucrezia Crivelli, and had refused to give her up. Wounded in her feelings and in her pride, Beatrice had pretended to see nothing in order to preserve her own happiness intact, and she had mastered her pain with great strength of spirit. She was pregnant for the third time, and by dint of will power she managed to save appearances, laughing, singing, arranging, commanding. On January 2, 1497, she held a ball in her apartments, with the whole court present. Toward evening she was taken ill; she was carried to her bedchamber; at two o'clock that morning she gave birth to a stillborn son, and within an hour and a half she died.

The chronicles of all Italy were filled with accounts of Lodovico's immoderate, theatrical, and romantic grief, of his repentant self-reproaches, his passionate lamentings, of the funeral at Santa Maria della Grazie in the midst of a thousand flaming torches and thousands upon thousands of wax tapers, and of the final appearance of Beatrice robed in gold upon her bier. The blinding suddenness of the misfortune had moved everyone; and those twenty-two years consumed with such intensity and fervor had, it seemed, upheld not only the fortunes of the Sforza family but also the destiny of the duchy. From the moment of Beatrice's death, the future of Milan began to cloud; soon after followed the French invasions, the fall of the Sforza, and the imprisonment of Lodovico, who was fated to die in exile, in the castle of Loches.

Isabella's sorrow, like her character, was genuine but controlled. Having shed her tears, she kept assiduously in touch with her brother-in-law, feeling for Il Moro—powerful and superstitious, fanciful and realistic, indecisive and stubborn as he was—the attraction that strong, clear-headed women feel for men who are full of self-contradictions and, when all is said, are weak. She recovered quickly from her grief, for she had to ward off the perils represented by the French flanking her to the north, Cesare Borgia threatening from the south, papal interventions, and the bitter hostility of the Venetians. With disdainful patience she endured a family tie with the Borgia when, in 1501, with the Borgia star in full ascendancy, Lucrezia married her brother Alfonso d'Este, the widower of Anna Sforza, and came to reign in Ferrara as its Duchess.

To Cesare Borgia she sent masks, perfumes, and compliments to hold him at bay; at the same time she exulted when the troops of Faenza successfully withstood the Borgia forces, which led her to formulate her clear concept of domestic policy: the prince must deserve to have the people make his cause their own by making their cause his. This was the traditional Este idea of good government and, joined with a feminine nature, it was now translated into a series of sustained, sensitive political moves. All Mantua acknowledged the efficacy of Isabella's policies during her regency in 1509, a period when the League of Cambrai united

Europe in an alliance against the excessive power of Venice. It
so happened that Francesco Gonzaga, commander for the league,
was taken prisoner while he was sleeping, to the anger and dis-
gust of his allies. The little Mantuan state faced a grave danger
then, but Isabella demonstrated her courage and the growth of
her personality by calling the people together, offering her young
son for the public's acclamation, and enjoining the strictest orders
upon the army—forbidding the garrisons of the fortresses border-
ing Venice to open their gates even were the Venetians to lead
Marquis Francesco to the foot of the glacis and murder him before
their eyes.

And so Francesco Gonzaga, languishing and ill in Venetian
prisons, waited to be liberated while, in Mantua, Isabella played
a most artful hand. Caught in a fearsome vise between venomous
foes and suspicious friends, she succeeded in keeping the Mantuan
frontier free not only of enemy assaults but also of allied garrisons.
But because she had governed too well and ably, she found in
1512, the war ended, that she had lost the love of her husband.
Shortly after his return from prison, Francesco Gonzaga wrote her
in these words: *"We are ashamed* that it is our fate to have as
wife a woman who is always ruled by her head." Not at all in-
timidated, Isabella replied with icy pride: "Your Excellency is
indebted to me as never husband was to wife; nor must Your
Excellency think that, even did you love and honor me more than
any person in the world, you could repay my good faith." Day
after day she watched as her husband became increasingly alien-
ated. When she sensed that she had fallen from power, she protested in a way all her own—not in words but in action. She
traveled, and one of her destinations was Rome.

Isabella arrived in Rome like a reigning sovereign who was
securely established in her own kingdom. No one suspected her
real situation. In the splendid company of the papal court of
Leo X, surrounded by the continuous thunder of acclamation,
amid all the banquets and theatricals and the penetrating, brilliant
talk, she permitted no one to guess the contrast between such
homage and her true vagrant isolation. She was buoyed up by her

taste for experimentation, and the thought of her children helped her—the sons, that is, who must be guided toward great futures. (Her daughters she cared very little about—at least at this time. When two of them, Ippolita and Paola, entered a convent, she did not weep, but with a license verging on blasphemy, declared herself content, since this son-in-law would cause her no trouble.) Her sons, Federigo, Ercole, and Ferrante, were educated and watched over with daily, unremitting attention. The first was destined to the throne, the second to the Church, the third to the army. But Federigo was clearly her favorite; her affection for him was the supreme expression of her maternal love, her pride, and even a kind of hope in the future. This explains how she could separate from the husband who had stripped her of all authority, for she knew that in Federigo she had a future, and she planned her own vindication in that future. When Francesco Gongaza died in 1519, worn down by illness, Isabella's tears paid tribute only to the memories of her youth. Since her son was far away in France, the one urgent and essential thing for her to do was to rule.

It was 1519, Isabella was forty-four, and to reign was the natural expression of her nature. "She trusts no one and will know the motive of everyone," observed the Mantuans, who were never displeased to have power exercised by a woman of her sort of matriarchal nobility.

Federigo, the nineteen-year-old Marquis, was at first overwhelmed by his mother and lived in a state of admiring subjugation, with little more than the occasional restiveness of an unruly colt. She governed well; she maintained a difficult equilibrium among the great powers that divided Italy, and she was the first to foresee that Charles V would prevail over the French King, Francis I. But Federigo presently discovered that his life was partitioned into two roles: one, that of the submissive son, and the other his own, that of an independent, effective man. It was only natural that the second seemed to him the good and true self, all the more so since he had the support of a young and extremely beautiful woman in proving it. The Young Marquis was so in love with Isabella Boschetti, called La Boschetta, that he refused to marry to ensure the continuity of the dynasty. The young woman fueled Federigo's idea of his total independence, and he responded by surrounding her with every royal honor, costly and magnificent gifts, courtiers, artists, and literary figures, while by sly, imperceptible moves he eliminated his mother little by little from direct participation in the government. He asked her advice, but privately—and gradually Isabella was relegated to the role of an elderly woman.

No moment in her life had been so serious as this, and once again she bided her time, waiting for her son's mistress to fall from favor. Isabella was coming to recognize bitterly that her beloved Federigo was a weak man, and worse. "The Marquis of Mantua is not good for much," Guicciardini wrote with terse accuracy in 1527, when Federigo and the Duke of Urbino opened the way by their betrayal for the German mercenaries to march south to sack the city of Rome.

Isabella d'Este had returned to Rome in 1525, and so shared in the final days of that tempered, cultivated, Christian paganism that was to be shattered by the brutal impact of the Lutheran gangs from Frundsberg. Rome had received her gloriously in the time of Leo X, and now, under another Medici, Clement VII, it welcomed her again. And again Isabella stood firm in her loyalty to Mantua and to the Gonzaga who had so often betrayed her. Thanks to her subtly modulated tactics, she succeeded in securing the red hat for her second son, Ercole, only a few days before the dreadful pillage of the city began. Federigo was writing her from Mantua meanwhile. He had seen the imperial hordes at first hand, and found them crude, fanatical, blasphemous, and innately hostile to the soil and civilization of Italy. Again and again he begged his mother to return to Mantua, but these entreaties had the opposite effect: they suggested a strengthening of her position that might restore her to an ascendancy over her son far above the poor physical expedients of La Boschetta. And then the terrible day, May 6, 1527, arrived. From within Palazzo Colonna, where she was securely housed, she heard the mercenaries howling through the streets, bent on robbing, killing, and torturing. Isabella remained steadfast; she took in gentlewomen, princes, ambassadors, priests, and friars who were seeking shelter; she encouraged them, shared her meager food with them, and with them trembled and hoped. Only when they were out of danger did she leave the ravaged city and make her way northward to Mantua without undue haste. Fired by the evidences of her courage, the populace was all for her and against La Boschetta. And gradually La Boschetta had to give in, retreat, and remove herself, allowing Federigo to marry Princess Margherita Paleologa—the wife chosen for him by Isabella.

Margherita was gentle, sensible, and in love; she had just the right degree of native shrewdness; and as her dowry she brought with her nothing less than a whole region—Monferrato. She bore her husband numerous sons, gave him constant, discreet support, and got along extremely well with her great mother-in-law, who gladly placed full confidence in her. Federigo's political future was a limited one, subject as it was to the will of Charles V, but within the sphere of his large and splendid court he was active, buying painting and sculpture, building extensively with his Giulio Romano, quarreling with his Aretino. Toward the mother to whom he owed so much, including his title of Duke, which Charles V granted to the rulers of Mantua, he continued to behave courteously and even affectionately, but he persisted in keeping her isolated. Her greatness of spirit was truly tried, yet her response was a gesture generous to the point of scorn; in effect, she offered to be his accomplice against her own interests, helping him to conceal her humiliation so that no one could suspect him of an unworthy action.

The futures of the other sons had been secured. Ferrante, the future Viceroy of Milan, would be a good general. Ercole would be a great cardinal, a major figure at the Council of Trent, and would come very near to wearing the triple crown; and when his elder brother died at barely forty years of age, leaving an infant heir, he would assume the regency of the duchy of Mantua and perform his duties with the prudence, the severity, and the awareness of his mother.

Although no one needed Isabella now, as she moved into her sixtieth year, she was stronger and more animated and gay than ever, always ready and eager to go to the heart of a problem. Respect and consideration were paid her in abundance; her court was, as always, exemplary and, as always, crowded with literary figures, courtiers, and beautiful and witty young women whom she formed and trained in her own school according to her own bold and modern moral concept—allowing them freedom but insisting that they be virtuous. In her new apartments on the ground floor of the ducal palace, she collected about her the noblest and finest creations that her age was producing. The famous rooms, the *Studiolo* and the *Grotta* with the celebrated door by Tullio Lombardo, were the talk of all the courts of Italy. Poems, songs, travel memoirs, writings of every description, flowed into Mantua from all over to satisfy her ever livelier curiosity. Nor did the heavy traffic in elegant luxuries diminish—the gowns, jewels, perfumes, cosmetics, adornments, and extraordinary objects like the doll "dressed inside and out exactly like her [Isabella]," which Francis I requested and received to send to his wife in France. But above all this, Isabella's inner life was fortified by a secret. This secret was called Solarolo.

Solarolo was a tiny possession in Romagna that belonged to her. This was all Isabella needed. She received secretaries as if they were ministers; she directed and adjudicated and enforced her own methods of management with almost affectionate ease, since here she was legitimately fulfilling her true nature and was finally giving expression to the passion for ruling that could have made her a magnificent queen. As she listened to her secretaries' reports, with the maps of Solarolo spread before her, and around her her collections of paintings, marbles, bronzes both ancient and modern, her crystal and her alabaster and her ornate clocks, she was expressing her personality fully and harmoniously.

Most rare Phoenix, the humanists called her, reviving the worn image to honor her—but more than that, a most rare woman. Yet why does posterity remember her? In both her marriage and her maternity she was sorely disappointed; emotionally hers was a wintry life. She has survived thanks to her individuality, to the

awareness of self that she sustained with all the force and conviction of a style. It was a style fashioned by the mind; it was
the effective alliance of idea and action; and it characterized
Isabella's life until her death on February 13, 1539. It is impossible
to say whether Beatrice would have been able to develop in the
same way, had she lived to the same age. But both these princesses,
these creatures of lucid and resolute intelligence, had understood
one thing—the necessity of living according to an inner order that
vibrates in continual response to the external world, and by
which we surmount the error of facts, the harshness of circumstance, and the inertia of our surroundings.

Translated by Adrienne Foulke

Index